Minding Your CyberManners on the Internet

by Donald Rose, Ph.D.

alpha
books

A Division of Macmillan Publishing
A Prentice Hall Macmillan Company
201 West 103rd Street, Indianapolis, Indiana, 46290

For my parents, Jean and Ben, and my brother Robert, with thanks for all their love and support.

© **1994 Alpha Books**

All rights reserved. No part of this book shall be reproduced, stored in a retrieval system, or transmitted by any means, electronic, mechanical, photocopying, recording, or otherwise, without written permission from the publisher. No patent liability is assumed with respect to the use of the information contained herein. Although every precaution has been taken in the preparation of this book, the publisher and author assume no responsibility for errors or omissions. Neither is any liability assumed for damages resulting from the use of the information contained herein. For information, address Alpha Books, 201 W. 103rd Street, Indianapolis, IN 46290.

International Standard Book Number:1-56761-521-X
Library of Congress Catalog Card Number: 94-72482

96 95 94   8 7 6 5 4 3 2 1

Interpretation of the printing code: the rightmost number of the first series of numbers is the year of the book's printing; the rightmost number of the second series of numbers is the number of the book's printing. For example, a printing code of 94-1 shows that the first printing of the book occurred in 1994.

Screen reproductions in this book were created by means of the program Collage Plus from Inner Media, Inc., Hollis, NH.

Printed in the United States of America

Publisher
Marie Butler-Knight

Acquisitions Editor
Barry Pruett

Managing Editor
Elizabeth Keaffaber

Product Development Manager
Faithe Wempen

Senior Development Editor
Seta Frantz

Production Editor
Phil Kitchel

Copy Editor
Barry Childs-Helton

Tech Editors
Wayne Blankenbeckler and Art Smoot

Cover Designer
Jay Corpus

Designer
Carol Stamile

Indexer
Rebecca Mayfield

Production Team
Dan Caparo, Brad Chinn, Kim Cofer, Lisa Daugherty,
David Dean, Cynthia Drouin, Jennifer Eberhardt,
David Garratt, Erika Millen, Beth Rago,
Bobbi Satterfield, Karen Walsh, Robert Wolf

Contents

Part I Plunging In: The Basics of CyberManners

1 Electronic Mail: Primary Mode of Online Interaction   3

What Is Electronic Mail, and
Why Do I Need It? 3
How to Compose a Standard
E-mail Message 5
Embellishments: Useful
Abbrev's & "Cyberese" 7
More Embellishments: Expressing
Emotions in E-mail 12
Summary Points (These Will Be
on the Midterm) 15

2 Cybercommandments: Do's and Don'ts of E-mail Manners   17

Why You Need Good E-mail Manners 17
To E-mail or Not to E-mail:
When to Use It 18
Some General Rules of Thumb
for E-mail Manners 21
Rules for More Specific E-mail Tasks 35
How to Learn More About
E-mail Manners 38
Summary Points 39

3 Using USENET and Virtual Global Bulletin Boards   41

What Are Virtual Bulletin Boards and
the Ubiquitous USENET? 41
How to Compose a Standard
Bboard Message 42
Embellishments: Some Bboard Cyberese ... 43
Get the Meaning 45
Summary Points 48

4 Cybercommandments II: Do's and Don'ts of Bboard Manners — 49

Why You Need Good
  Bboard Manners 49
Some General Rules of Thumb for
  Bboard Manners 50
How to Learn More About
  Bboard Manners 66
Q & A on Bboard Manners 67
Summary Points 70

5 More Manners Matters: Do's and Don'ts for Other Cybertasks — 71

Should It Stay or Should It Go:
  Managing Mailbox Messages 72
A Place for My Stuff: Managing
  Disk Storage 72
Net Navigation: Rules for Telnet 73
Shifting Bits: Rules for File Transfers 74
Mailing-list Discussion Groups 76
Summary Points 78

Part II Popular Problems and Questionable Net Behavior

6 Flaming: When Messages Get Too Emotional or Negative — 81

Some Flame Basics 82
What Causes Flames? 82
Advice for Dealing with Flames 84
Flame Retardants: Protecting
  Yourself Against the Heat 87
When You Too Get the Urge to Flame… ... 88
Flame in a Box: the Semi-official
  Standard Flame Form 90
Flame in a Box II: My Own Version 92
Summary Points 92

Contents

7 Spamming, Jamming, and Whamming, Oh My! More Cyberproblems   **93**

   Spamming: Mass Postings 94
   Jamming: Overcrowding E-mailboxes
      and Bboards 96
   Whamming: Harsh Reaction Tactics 101
   Summary Points 102

8 "Do You Know Me?": Interesting Net Personality Types   **103**

   Anonymous Versus Famous: Real
      and Fake Identities on the Net 104
   The Clark-to-Superman Effect:
      When the Shy Turn Bold 105
   The Jekyll and CyberHyde Effect:
      When the Nice Turn Mean 107
   Bitpickers: Netters Who Nitpick,
      Overdetail, or Overanalyze 108
   Funny Fiends: Those Who Overdo
      Humor and How to Deal with Them 109
   Info Addicts: "Get Away
      From That Tube!" Revisited 110
   The Gump Effect: "Stupid Is as
      Stupid Does" on the Net 112
   Robocomm: Automated Agents Online ... 114
   Summary Points 115

Part III Going Deeper

9 Cybertalk and Virtual Sex: Interactive Interchange on the Net   **119**

   Chat Chic: Virtual Orality and
      Online Cybertalk 119
   How Cybertalk Compares to
      Real-world Talking 120
   Some Manners Rules for
      General Cybertalk 121

      Reach Out and Touch Some Fun:
         Cybersex Chat 124
      Rules for Cybersex Chat
         and Scoring Virtual Touch(downs) 125
      Q & A on Cyberdating and Net Love 130
      Summary Points 131

10 Gender Issues in Cyberspace 133
      Advantages of Cyberspace (Versus
         Real-life) Communication for Women ... 134
      Advice Regarding Online
         Gender Issues 135
      Q & A 137
      Summary Points 138

11 Making Friends and Fostering Community in Cyberspace 139
      Background 139
      Advice for Finding Friends Online 141
      Advice for Fostering Community
         Online 141
      Summary Points 142

12 Net Privacy and Account Protection 143
      Background 143
      Examples and Anecdotes:
         Privacy Matters 144
      Some Rules for Enhancing Your Online
         Privacy and Protection 145
      Summary Points 148

13 Virtual Ventures: Working, Advertising, and Profiting Online 149
      Cybermanners Related
         to Your Work Life 150
      Manners Rules for Net Advertising
         and Commercial Success 152
      Q & A 156
      Summary Points 158

14	**Cybercensorship**	**159**
	Some Censorship Background	159
	Some Anecdotes to Learn From	160
	Summary Points	162
15	**Nethics: Ethical Issues on the Net**	**163**
	Background	163
	Nethics Rules	165
	Q & A	166
	Summary Points	168

Part IV Reference

Appendix A The Hall of Flame — 171
   The Form Flame: Another View 171
   Voted "Most Likely to Be Flamed":
     Top Seven Examples of Flame Bait 173

Appendix B Cyberese — 175
   Acronyms and Abbreviations 175
   Emoticons 178

Glossary The Neat Net Set — 181

Index — 191

Introduction

Why You Need This Book!

Imagine being told you couldn't use your local telephone service anymore because of some calls you made. Not told by your Mom or spouse, mind you—but by the telephone service itself. Hard to believe? Think again. You *can* get kicked off your phone service; for example, Canada now has a strict direct-marketing law, and one company that abused it found its phone service cut off! But don't get paranoid—this probably won't happen to you (you've paid your bills, right?). However, something like this *is* happening to certain people around the country, who are misusing a newly popular medium called the Internet.

There is a comparison to be drawn between the phone company and the Internet—you can get away with a lot, but there are some definite no-no's and some "common" rules of courtesy that you *should* follow. This book deals with these issues, among other things. In general, it helps if you, the reader, understand that these are not arbitrary rules or the whims of contrary people on the net—*there are certain cultures that need to be respected and understood*, just as there are in other countries, on campuses, in different regions of the U.S., with different ethnic groups, and so on.

But I hear some of you say, "What *is* the Internet?" Is the name actually short for "INcredibly TERrific NETwork"? No, I made that up; but such a description does do it justice. In reality (or virtual reality, if you prefer), the Internet is a global "network of networks" that connects about 25 to 30 million "netters" residing in hundreds of cities. (Speaking of cities, there are approximately as many netters as the populations of New York City and Paris combined. Just an interesting fact to put the millions in perspective.)

The Internet and related services allow users to communicate in many ways—which we'll discuss in detail in this very book. Although scientific, educational, and government groups have used the Internet since the '70s, usage has increased dramatically in recent years; approximately 2 million folks per month are now getting hooked up to it, and hooked on it.

Introduction

But why do some folks get forced off this medium? Because of *improper conduct*. If these folks only knew of the basic rules for using the Internet *properly*, they might have avoided the hassle—and, in some cases, the embarrassment—of forced electronic exile. If you don't take steps to ensure you use the net properly and understand its rules of etiquette, you may start feeling that Internet stands for "INfuriating TERrifying NETwork." But do not fret, kind reader: This book is here to help you!

We all know many rules for proper conduct in real life, in many contexts. "Do the right thing. Don't be cruel. Be good to your neighbor. Do unto others as you'd have them do unto you. Mind your manners." Now the Internet and other online services have grown explosively into a "cyberverse" ("cybernetic universe")—another nickname, along with "cyberspace," "information superhighway," and "net," for electronic networks that connect people by mostly text-based communication. The key phrase here is "connect *people*"—those clever, ornery, social creatures. Internet users are finding they need to identify—and apply—proper behaviors too.

Minding Your CyberManners on the Internet will help you conduct yourself as an intelligent Internet individual, with the utmost discretion. I show you how to enjoy the useful features of the net without trampling any virtual toes. If you want to behave more like a true guru and avoid ineptness-induced brouhahas, you need this book. If you want a resource to help you figure out what proper conduct is so you and your friends don't get kicked off (or get others ticked off), this is it! Imagine an electronic morph of a slang dictionary and Emily Post, and you approach the spirit behind this volume. Your online coolness and correctness quotients will improve in several ways, helping your cyberstyle appear more like Miss Manners than "Dis Manners" (as in disruptive, disrespectful and disinterested in others).

Some readers might ask why they should bother to learn about manners when dealing with computers. Manners are for people, not machines, right? If you were communicating directly with a machine, perhaps that would be true (though don't tell that to intelligent androids like Commander Data). It bears repeating: the information superhighway is mainly about *connecting real people*.

A popular metaphor for the Internet is the telephone, which is also a machine used as a conduit to connect people. Believe it or not, in the early days of the telephone there were consultants who made a living advising phone users on manners and other issues surrounding how to use the new medium. Today, consultants are just as vital for users of the Internet and other online services. You, dear reader, are lucky enough to have an urbane and confidential consultant in the form of this book (just think how much money you've already saved)!

To further illustrate why you're brilliant to be drinking in the contents of this book, here are the semi-official...

Top 10 Reasons to Buy This Book:

10. You don't wanna be roadkill on the information superhighway (or even the information backroads).

9. You want people online to *read* your messages, not delete them automatically.

8. CyberRodneyDangerfields are uncool—you wanna get "respect" online.

7. "Shoplifting is a crime" says McGruff, that talking crime dog. If he weren't a cartoon, he'd buy this book.

6. You want to learn the correct way to approach your fave celebrity online.

5. You'll buy any book with the word "Internet" in the title.

4. You want to learn how to properly develop online relationships with other people who think like you—or think they like you.

3. You want to know how to respond online to people who *don't* think like you.

2. You're tired of getting nasty messages online due to your bad manners, and you don't even know what you're doing.

1. You already love me, think I speak with golden tongue, and want to support my writing career so I can write even more fun and informative books in the future. (Hey, thanks.)

Introduction

What Is and Isn't Covered

Here are some assumptions I've taken the liberty of making about you, the reader. Don't worry, I haven't been reading your e-mail or your mind; writers must often make assumptions in order to write coherently.

- I assume you are, to some degree, already familiar with the Internet.

- I assume you have heard about related online services such as CompuServe, PRODIGY, and America Online—the three biggest, not counting the behemoth Internet itself, which isn't a single unified service. The Internet has many popular synonyms, but I will usually refer to it as simply "the net," and in some contexts will use "net" to encompass other online services as well, since the majority are connected to the Internet in some fashion.

- I assume you have access to other books, articles, or manuals for finding specific details on what net services exist, comparing service features, getting online, solving the mysteries of hooking your computer to a modem, and so on. If you need a good book on this subject, try *The Complete Idiot's Guide to the Internet* and *The Complete IdiotÆs Next Step with the Internet*, both by Peter Kent; they're from Alpha Books, the same illustrious people who brought you this elegant volume. (Coincidence? I don't think so.) Otherwise, I assume you have experienced most of the more mundane nitty-gritty of getting onto the net and getting your hands wet, and are now ready to explore more subtle—yet equally important—issues of properly using it.

In short, the main focus of this book is on the *social and psychological* issues related to interactions in cyberspace.

Defining Cybermanners

What exactly are "cybermanners?" Learning how to arrange images of knives and forks correctly in a virtual dining room?

To quote John McLaughlin: "Wrong!"

Let's define "manners" first. Webster defines manners as "morals; social customs; breeding; social conduct." Roget adds "politeness." Certainly one strives to exhibit these qualities (one *is* civilized, isn't one?) when communicating in person, on the phone, or by letter—and so they should also apply to electronic communication. I'll be using, however, a broader definition for "cybermanners", covering the right and wrong ways to compose and distribute electronic messages, and examining how various classes of people deal with cyberspace—and interact in it.

Also note that different people have different opinions about what constitutes good and bad manners, whether in the cyber realm or not. No etiquette rules-of-thumb can please everyone.

So there are gradations, shades of nuance, along the spectrum between very bad cybermanners (such as unethical or illegal activity) and the very good. It's a fuzzy concept. This book will help "defuzzify" some of the shady areas for you. It addresses many areas along this spectrum, from intentionally offensive messages to accidental syntactic mistakes. By the end of these chapters, we will not have a definitive single answer to what perfect cybermanners are, but instead will have provided a roadmap along which you can navigate with confidence.

About the Author

Dr. Donald Rose, Ph.D., who has spent thousands of hours wandering the Internet, is a high-tech writer and lecturer who specializes in artificial intelligence. When he isn't glued to his monitor, he performs comedy (at the Improv and othe clubs) and writes plays.

Acknowledgments

Thanks to those writers who graciously allowed quotation or parapharsing of some of their ideas, especially Michael Strangelove. Another heaping helping of thanks to my agent, Matt Wagner, and to my friend and colleague Michael Utvich.

And finally, endless thanks for the love and friendship of Dr. Christine Kolar. I'll always be grateful for her support, her patience, her amazing cooking, and her warm smile which often came just at the right moment.

part I

Plunging In: The Basics of CyberManners

Congratulations, you've made it to Part One! In this part of the book, I will present the basic concepts and rules related to cybermanners—that is, those which are the most important for your "net life," and which will probably get the most use.

The first two chapters cover electronic mail (or "e-mail"), arguably the most utilized mode of online interactions. After what I call the Cybercommandments—which are not written in stone, I'm afraid, but are still a solid collection of do's and don'ts for e-mail manners.

I then turn to the topic of USENET and virtual global bulletin boards ("bboards" for short), which most netters can read as well as send messages to. Bboards often obey rules similar to those of e-mail; read on for more details of the differences, of course. As in the e-mail chapters, I cover the essentials of bboards first (in Chapter 3), then turn (in Chapter 4) to Cybercommandments II—more do's and don'ts, this time for bboard manners.

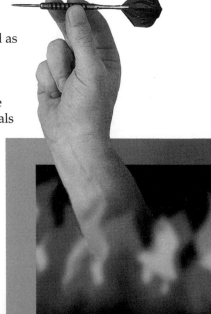

The last chapter in this part of the book presents more manners advice related to important cybertasks other than e-mail and bboards.

chapter 1

Electronic Mail: Primary Mode of Online Interaction

In This Chapter

We'll get into:

- ▐ Background about electronic mail communication on the net.
- ▐ The basics of composing messages in cyberspace.
- ▐ A collection of common abbreviations and other specialized words or phrases ("cyberese").
- ▐ Emoticons: one way to add more nuance to your net mail.

What Is Electronic Mail, and Why Do I Need It?

So you've gotten onto the Internet (or just "net," for us cyberhipsters). How do people communicate in this brave new world? One way is by sending messages that serve as the online analog of mail: electronic mail, or *e-mail*.

Imagine receiving and reading a letter right on your computer. Right on!—that's what receiving e-mail is like. Now imagine writing a letter on your online service (your "on-ramp" to the Internet, such as CompuServe, America Online, PRODIGY, or a smaller local service). You can send this as e-mail to anyone else on the Internet! Or, if you prefer, you can write a letter in your word processing program on your home computer, then upload it (transfer it from your computer to your net account via modem and communications software) and again send it as e-mail.

Once you have your account, you are given your Internet address. As in the U.S. mail system, everyone is given an address. If we didn't have addresses, the poor mail carriers would spend all their time searching the globe for us. It's the same with the Internet. Everyone must have an address so mail can flow smoothly from one person to another. My Internet address looks like this:

drose@pro-palmtree.socal.com

Don't fret; it may look like an indecipherable machine language, but you don't have to be an expert on net addresses to use one. Just think of it as a label on someone's electronic mailbox, or "e-mailbox." In this case, "drose" (Get it? *Donald Rose*?) is my online name or "handle," which is separated from my e-mailbox location by the "@" sign. (You need both a name *and* a location, just like real/physical mail does.) The location is usually two to four words separated by periods, which the Internet uses to figure out where to deposit your message. My e-mailbox is located on the "Pro-Palmtree" online service, which is itself located within "socal" (hip cyberese for Southern California) and is a commercial ("com") service.

Don't worry if the stuff after the "@" symbol seems like "Geek speak" to you right now. First of all, you'll get used to it, and it'll get easier to recognize and understand. Second, the most important task is to *get the spelling right*. For now it doesn't matter if you don't know what every part of your address means; as long as all the parts are correct in the "To:" field of your message, you'll be all right. (More on fields later!)

Why do you need e-mail? For one thing, it's the most common mode of communication on the net. E-mail also connects users of non-Internet services to the net, by using a "gateway" to shuttle messages between the net and the other services. Armed with your address, anyone on the net (or connected to it, such as through services like America Online, PRODIGY, or CompuServe) can send you a message. And you can send to any net address as well.

Plus, there may be times when you cannot reach someone with other media, or other media might not be as fast as e-mail. (For example, I know one person—he shall remain nameless—who rarely returns phone calls yet is very prompt in answering e-mail. And e-mail usually beats regular physical mail in speed, especially as the physical distance increases between sender and recipient.)

Since this book is about cybermanners, I'm not going to spend too much time on the basics of e-mail, but luckily there are two excellent and fun books that answer more detailed questions you may have about the subject: *The Complete Idiot's Guide to the Internet* and its follow-up, *The Complete Idiot's Next Step with the Internet*, both written by Peter Kent (no, he's not Clark's brother) and published by Alpha Books.

How to Compose a Standard E-mail Message

Just to give the most basic of the basics, let's quickly run through the proper syntax or format and content of messages—a quick refresher course in case you are new to e-mail and Kent's books are temporarily out of stock (Superman fans are a fanatical bunch).

If you're starting out, picture e-mail as just an electronic version of a standard letter. You write a letter in a word processing program; in most cases, you can use the special e-mail editor provided by your net account. After checking over the letter (some programs even have a spelling checker) and re-editing if needed, you send the letter to the net address you desire. You can even send copies to other addresses.

To illustrate, here's a hypothetical message from my own Internet account on the Pro-Palmtree service to my friend Mary's account at ACME-Net. Note that the first five lines of the message aren't really composed within the message—they're separate, in kind of the way an envelope (and its information) are separate from the actual ink-on-paper letter a person writes:

> Date: Wed, 20 Jul 94 15:18:38 PST
> From: drose (Donald Rose)
> To: mary@acme-net.com
> Cc: drose
> Subject: hi!
> how are you, for gosh sakes? I'm writing to you because my life sucks, I'm procrastinating on this CyberManners book again, and you've always been such a great waste of time for me :)
> Also, I miss your ugly mug :)
> Take care... You're my favorite human crutch. -Donald
> ———
> UUCP: hatch!pro-palmtree!drose   Pro-Palmtree BBS
> Inet: drose@pro-palmtree.socal.com 310-453-8726 v.32

First, notice the content (from "how are you" to "Donald"). You can put anything in an e-mail message that you'd write in a letter. Of course, there are special rules of manners for what kind of content you should and shouldn't put in e-mail, which I provide a bit later.

The top part (before the content) is the header. It carries relevant information about the message, a kind of meta-message. Its information includes who sent the message (the From: field or line); addresses to which this message will be delivered (To:); other addresses that will receive a "carbon copy" of the message (Cc:); the message subject; and the date of sending. An address can represent a person's mailbox, or the mailbox of a business or other group.

Also notice the information about myself and my Internet service provider at the end of the message. This section—the "signature" or "sig"—is automatically put at the end of every message by most mail programs. Not every mail program deals with signatures, but nearly every Internet-specific mail program will. Example: CompuServe users don't have a sig option when they're using their mail gateway to send e-mail to the Internet. In some systems, you have the power to create your own signature; on my Pro-Palmtree service, I just use the default sig.

Okay. Now you've seen an e-mail message. On a technical level, you can type anything that you would in a normal, physical letter. But what now? Am I going to tell you how to compose good e-mail? Reveal what a bad letter and a good letter look like? Of course. But first I will provide some information that should help streamline your messages, as well as help you understand others' messages. *Then* we'll get to do's and don'ts and rules of advice for e-mail—so be patient! (It's a virtue, you know, even in the virtual world!)

Embellishments: Useful Abbrev's & "Cyberese"

Saving time for readers as well as senders is one hallmark of proper cybermanners. To help achieve this, abbrev's (short for abbreviations—hey, that's self-referential!) are often used in place of commonly used words and phrases. However, there are certain *other* words and phrases that are also used frequently in net messages, in order to describe commonly encountered types of persons, things, situations, or other phenomena.

Together I call all these elements of net-related language *cyberese*. Note that you will often run across these new elements when reading your e-mail messages; in addition, they are in newsgroups and other forms of net communication as well. But (to partially quote Bobby McFerrin) don't worry; this new language will quickly become part of your life and second nature to use, IMHO (in my humble opinion).

Chapter 1

See, there's one already! Easy, right? Now here's some of the more common abbreviations you may encounter on the Internet:

IMNSHO	=	In My Not-So-Humble Opinion
IMO	=	In My Opinion (let's hear it for simplicity)
IMCO	=	In My Considered Opinion
IOW	=	In Other Words
OTOH	=	On The Other Hand
BTW	=	By The Way
FAQ	=	Frequently Asked Question(s)
YMMV	=	Your Mileage May Vary
WTH	=	What The Heck
FWIW	=	For What It's Worth
POV	=	Point Of View
RL	=	Real Life
FYI	=	For Your Information
FYA	=	For Your Amusement
BIF	=	Basis In Fact
NBIF	=	No Basis In Fact
ROTFL	=	Rolling On The Floor Laughing
RSN	=	Real Soon Now
MOTD	=	Message Of The Day
AKA	=	Also Known As (e.g., "Pres. Clinton AKA Mr. Bill")

Here are some others often seen online:

GR&D	=	Grinning Running & Ducking

ROTF,L	=	Rolling On The Floor, Laughing (note comma)
TIA	=	Thanks In Advance
TIC	=	Tongue In Cheek
[TM]	=	TradeMark
PC	=	Politically Correct (or Personal Computer, or IBM's PC, depending on context)
PI or PIC	=	Politically Incorrect
unPC	=	a cute way of saying the same thing as PI (also good to use if you are e-mailing a message to a Private Investigator)
RTM	=	Read The Manual (or Message)

And of course, although you can't see colors on most net systems today, let's not forget the bluer side of language (yes, it still exists in cyberspace—some say even more frequently):

RTFM	=	Read The F***ing Manual (or message)—or, Read That Fine Manual (yeah, right!)
PITA	=	Pain In The A**
BTSOOM	=	Beats The S**t Out Of Me—or, Beats The Snot Out Of Me (sure!)
FUBAR	=	F****d Up Beyond All Recognition (a military classic)
SNAFU	=	Situation Normal, All F****d Up (another military classic)
NFW	=	No F***ing Way

Some of these are in more common use than others, RTM and RTFM are universally acknowledged. (If asked, you can say that F stands for "fine" or "friendly" or "fouled." But, as one netter said to anutter: "NFW!")

Note that when abbrev's stand in part for "cuss words" they are providing an interesting service. To the new netters or the very young, or ultraconservatives, they appear harmless and do not overtly offend anyone. But for those "in the know," they get the intent across (strong emotion, the usual reason for cussing) without actually using any "politically incorrect" words (PO'd but not PI?).

Get the idea? The more used a phrase is, the more likely someone has abbrev'd it.

Now let's turn to net-unique words and phrases. The Glossary in the back has more terms, but for now, here's a sampling of some words having relevance to e-mail manners:

> **Newbie** New netter. Is sometimes more widely used for someone who either *is* new to the cyberworld, or just *acts* like s/he is. For example, someone may refer to you as a newbie in an e-mail message even if you've been online for months or years. Multiply the number of months you've been on the net *times* the number of "newbie" references you receive from others; the result is what I call your *embarrassment factor* (and—ahem—the number of times you should read this book :-))

> (Confidential to newbies: the previous entry ends with a "smiley," not a typo. To decipher this ancient symbol, read on.)

> **Flame** An emotional, often personal attack on another person's article. "I disagree with your statement because of X" is not a flame, but "I disagree with your moronic statement and the fact that you would say such a thing proves you're a complete idiot" is.

> **Flaming** Sending someone a flame (as in: "Hey, kind sir, instead of flaming everyone all the time, why don't you get a life?"—which itself may lead to more flaming, so forget this example).

Flame war When flames start firing back and forth between two or more netters—either via e-mail, or over bulletin boards (which is an even more flammable situation).

PC or PCness Politically correct and political correctness. (I will ignore PC's "personal computer" interpretation for a moment.) PCness has in recent years gathered a strong following, but even more recently has led to a strong backlash as well, especially on the net, which often seems more unPC, or PI. Like any democracy, the net's population is composed of various factions that have differing opinions; in some areas, PCness seems mandatory, while others (say, some forums on the extreme left or right, politically) may treat you strangely if you act that way. Sending a PC message is your safest bet, while acting PI is more likely to attract flaming behavior. But you must use your judgment.

Signature (AKA **sig** or **.sig**) A short, standardized message tacked onto the end of all one's posts; usually consisting of one to four lines of text, containing one's e-mail address, employer, favorite quote, and/or other pertinent (or impertinent) personal information. For a sig example, see my earlier message to Mary in this chapter.

Snailmail (AKA **Snail Mail**) The real-world analog to e-mail; the normal through-rain-and-snow postal service. (Snail implies slow, in case you're slow; but now I know you're in the know!)

Sie Gender-neutral pronoun equivalent to "She or He". Another way to convey the same intent: "s/he." Gender neutrality is usually considered PC on the net.

Hir Gender-neutral pronoun equivalent to "Him or Her," or possessive-pronoun equivalent to "His or Her" (alternate spelling: "Zie" and "Zir").

There are so many more examples of abbrev's and cyberese I can't list them all here; a more complete list

Chapter 1

appears in the Glossary. Besides, I know you are all sensitive souls, and can't wait to learn more about emotions in e-mail. Trust me, you will.

More Embellishments: Expressing Emotions in E-mail

In general, it is good cybermanners to express yourself as clearly as you can when you create online messages. Because the net is inherently a text medium, it lacks many of the nuances of ordinary face-to-face conversation—like facial expressions and tone of voice—so people try to make up for the lack in various ways. Fortunately, there are tools to help you do just that. Some of these tools are those strange combinations of punctuation marks you often see in people's messages—called *emoticons*.

Specifically, they are symbols created by arranging characters into a meaningful picture. Often they must be read sideways to be understood. For example, here is the most common type of emoticon, the "smiley face" or *smiley* :-) which can be seen best by tilting your head to the left 90 degrees. (Or, if you're really smart, you'll turn the book sideways.)

Why draw a picture sideways? Because if you don't, pictures can be more difficult to compose, can take up several lines, and too much of your time. For example, here is another smiley-faced person (with a crewcut added), to be read downward (i.e., normally):

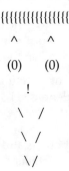

The first smiley is a lot quicker to write, and (surprise!) it's used a lot more often in the body of messages than the second kind. More complex pictures like the second example do often appear in signatures, however, since a user only needs to create a sig once; after that, it's included automatically in messages over and over, without additional time and expense required.

Emoticons evolved because they help make up for the lack of expressive power in net-based messages. They help increase the chance that your message will be understood properly, that you will convey the meaning you intend to get across. Such features are, of course, important to good manners online.

For example, you may make a statement that you feel is an obvious joke or something not to be taken too seriously (such as, "I'm always right, why bother arguing?" or something similar) in an e-mail message, but you cannot guarantee that the reader of your message will take the same view. Believe it or not, not everyone has the same inferencing rules. In particular, people rarely share the exact same sense of humor. (Ask any comedian.)

Hence, netters developed symbol combinations to help convey humor, such as the smiley face just shown. In fact, I added a smiley :) in my earlier sample message, after "ugly mug," to make sure Mary realized I was kidding about her face. Smileys are the most popular of the little pictogram emoticons, in part because they are so valuable. Let's face it :) ever notice how everyone thinks they're a comedian (once a day, at least)? No matter how broad the humor or satire, it is safer to remind people that you *are* being funny (or at least trying to be). So use the smiley and its variants to point out sections of articles with humorous intent.

Standard smileys include:

:-)	smile, smiley, or happy face (indicating humor)
:)	a noseless smiley (or *sans nose* in Frenglish)

Chapter 1

:.)	a small-skewed-button-nosed smiley
8-)	wide-eyed smile, or smile of one wearing glasses, which could also be **B-)**
:->	ironic or devious smile
;-)	yet another happy face (winking, which means there may be a devilish side to your words)
:-(	the anti-smiley (frown, that is; let down; sad)
>:-(	someone mad or annoyed
:-()	a big mouth (e.g., when you feel you rambled on)
:-O	surprised face (or a big mouth, or Mick Jagger)
@>—,—'-	a rose (sometimes useful in virtual dating)
xxooxxoo	love & kisses (also great for date mail)

There's an ongoing debate as to whether smileys are a good thing or a bad thing. Some people like to use them whenever possible, others feel that writing should stand on its own without having to point out whether something was supposed to be funny or not.

If you don't want your reader to develop a pain in the neck, another common means of conveying a smile without forcing a head tilt is by writing <G>, usually at the end of a sentence (G being short for Grin).

In fact, there are many variations used when composing emoticons, limited only by your ability to navigate the keyboard and tap into your spatial skills. Here is a sampling of some other emoticons:

You get the idea. There are just too many variations of emoticons to list them all here, but that's part of the fun; you can experiment with your keyboard and a blank screen. Extra points for getting the most "meaning added" or "nuance value" (as opposed to "nuisance value") from your emoticons while using the least number of characters.

Summary Points (These Will Be on the Midterm)

- Electronic mail is, for most users, the most commonly used feature of the net.

- The letter metaphor helps one understand how e-mail works.

- Certain abbreviations, words, and phrases—which I refer to as "cyberese"—have evolved on the net, language often used in online messages as a means to save time. Perhaps cyberese also evolved as a kind of in-the-know slang that was bound to happen, something which any clique (real or virtual) is likely to develop as part of tribal custom and culture.

- The emoticon is another form of communication information unique to the net. These friendly creatures help clarify meaning in messages.

While clarity is certainly one step on the road to excellent cybermanners, the next chapter takes you even farther. So far: one small step for man. Next: one giant leap for kind manners.

chapter 2

Cybercommandments: Do's and Don'ts of E-mail Manners

In This Chapter

Thus far we have discussed the basics to get you going in online messaging. Now that you can build and understand messages ...

- I will discuss why e-mail manners are necessary.
- Next I'll present rules-of-thumb for deciding when e-mail is the best medium of communication, and when it is not.
- Finally, I will delve into the heart of e-mail manners: rules for proper e-mail construction and usage.

Why You Need Good E-mail Manners

If you're still in doubt about why it's essential, please read these reasons. If not, read 'em anyway!

You could hurt someone's feelings. You may be trying to be funny, but if the person receiving your e-mail doesn't get your brand of humor, it can be misunderstood—even taken as an insult. And such misunderstandings can be compounded by the next maxim:

One mistake can be noticed by millions. (Not to give you stage fright, but…) a message can be forwarded to millions of people all over the Internet and connected services, or posted on a public electronic bulletin board ("bboard") read by people around the world (see later chapters for more on bboards). You wouldn't pick your nose on the Letterman show, would you? Well, a mistake in cyberspace can be "seen" by nearly as many people.

Cyberspace mistakes can affect your real-world interactions. If you turn someone off in an e-mail message, that person may decide to avoid you on the phone or in paper letters as well.

Just trust me! There are many other reasons, but I can't wait to share the great rules that are waiting in the wings, so I'm cutting right to them!

To E-mail or Not to E-mail: When to Use It

OK, not quite yet. The main Cybercommandments will just have to wait awhile longer. (Remember how long Moses took to get the real ones? Be patient!) First, let's make sure using e-mail at all is the cool thing to do.

Sometimes just using e-mail itself can cause problems, or simply may not be your best option, regardless of what your message contains. How does one know when to use it? Before sending net messages, you should at least consider using alternative media. Here are some rules of thumb to help you decide when e-mail is the best choice.

Ma Bell or Snail Mail Instead

▐▌ Really rushed? Use the phone.

The most urgent messages are almost always better sent via phone, since that provides the best chance of getting an immediate and fast dialog going. A phone is also more likely to get someone's immediate attention, since it rings, while e-mail is almost always received silently.

▐▌ Need non-textual nuance? Find a phone.

Sometimes you want to know as much about the other party as you can, perhaps needing to gauge voice inflection, hesitation or confidence, and so on. The phone conveys more subtle cues than e-mail in nearly all cases.

▐▌ Need fast, continuous interaction with someone? Phone again.

Current e-mail simply is not as interactive as phone calls today. For example, suppose it's the last day before you leave on vacation, and you want to check with your secretary one last time. Using e-mail, you run the risk that you will get no response before you depart, and any questions your secretary needs to ask may get to your e-mailbox *after* you leave.

▐▌ Use snailmail or phone if you face flakiness.

In your recipient's online service, that is. A service may be down (unavailable) for a period of time, or bouncing your messages back for any number of reasons (if e-mail cannot be delivered, it is usually "returned to sender," to quote the King). If you are explicitly told about such system flakiness, or suspect it (for example, you get some messages returned automatically), then avoid e-mail. Or cover your bases by sending e-mail *and* messages via other media.

▐▌ Recipient rarely reads e-mail? Use snail mail.

For example, it might be better to write than to e-mail a user like Tolstoy . (Dead writers rarely check their e-mail.)

▮▮▮ Message as long as *War and Peace*? Snailmail, don't e-mail, if the message is E X T R E M E L Y long, or is full of graphics and formatting.

Graphics and formatting information still cannot be processed correctly by most e-mail systems today (they show up as garbage at best). Also, most people don't like using a computer screen to read 100-page documents, or have these monsters clogging up their e-mailboxes (though it *is* possible to send and receive them, if—for some remote reason—there's no alternative). Finally, some online services will not let you store or send extremely large pieces of e-mail.

Also, long online files can be sent with specialized file transfer programs such as Internet's FTP (file transfer protocol, discussed a bit later). Remember: the longer your message, the less likely it will be read.

▮▮▮ Don't use e-mail to break up with someone.

Especially if they don't check their e-mail a lot. Besides, it's tacky. "Dear John" e-mail is even worse than "Dear John" letters.

Go for E-mail

▮▮▮ If your message is not overly long, use e-mail rather than the phone to send detailed or structured messages.

Documents, for example. It's awkward to recite a ten-page report over the phone. It is also easier and faster to scan an e-mail document than to rewind-and-fast-forward an answering machine (or voice-mail message) over and over again.

▮▮▮ Prefer e-mail when contacting famous folk or the overly busy and hard-to-reach.

These types are unlikely to either answer a phone or return calls promptly. Besides, in many cases, you will only have their e-mail address and not a phone number. Finally, you will probably get (and send) a more thought-out message by e-mail than by phone.

▉ Use e-mail when you want to compose the clearest message possible, yet avoid any delays that regular mail could cause.

You can gather, organize, manipulate, and store your thoughts much more easily with e-mail than with a phone call. But you'll usually get a reply before a regular-mail letter would even be received.

▉ In general, use the medium people ask you to use, or avoid those they tell you to avoid.

You may be told not to call someone at work, but what if you have to contact them? If they have e-mail access at work, you can send them an e-mail message, and you have not violated their request. However, if someone specifically asks you to *call* them back, for example, it is good manners to do so.

Some General Rules of Thumb for E-mail Manners

Okay, assume you've considered other media and have concluded that e-mail is the way to go for you. Here are some rules for e-mail cybermanners that should apply for any message you send.

The advice in this remarkably compact section was drawn from several sources—the best and brightest from around the globe. In addition to my own experience and insights, some of the following came from—or were inspired by—the net itself.

But enough preliminary talk, it's time to pump you up—on cybermanners rules for e-mail!

Before You Write: Pondering Your Reader, Yourself, and Your Image

"Think before you write" is good advice in *any* medium, and certainly applies to e-mail construction. Think about your goals, how your message helps or hinders you in attaining

21

them, and how others are likely to react to your e-mail. Some more specific rules of thumb are now presented.

- Remember: the person on the other side is human.

  Even if you think the person you're writing to acts more like a Klingon, you still should follow this rule. Interacting with the network through a computer makes it easy to forget that there are people "out there." Situations arise where emotions erupt into a verbal free-for-all that can lead to hurt feelings. (Those who can't figure out why hurt feelings are to be avoided probably aren't reading this book, or any other discussion of manners. Do them the courtesy of avoiding them.)

  Please remember that people all over the world might eventually read your words (if part of your e-mail is forwarded to others, or quoted in *another* person's e-mail). Do not attack people if you cannot persuade them with your presentation of the facts. Screaming, cursing, and abusing others only serves to make people think less of you, and magically renders them less willing to help you when you need it.

  If you are upset at something or someone, wait until you've had a chance to calm down and think about it. A cup of coffee or a good night's sleep works wonders on your perspective. Hasty words create more problems than they solve. Try not to say anything to others you would not say to them in person in a room full of people.

- Target the right audience.

  When you send an e-mail message, think about the person (or persons) you are trying to reach. For example, asking your professor of mathematics about the latest Stones record may seem innocuous, but it may be telling the prof that you don't value their time, which could turn that person off to you—even to the point where they refuse to answer any of your later questions (which may be much more important to you, such as whether integrals will be on the final exam).

Use the information you have about your audience. If your prof actually told you s/he is a Stones fan, then a Stones-related message may be OK—but if you lack any specific info like this, assume that people are busy, and probably will only answer questions that are relevant to the relationship you have with them (in this case, a student-teacher relationship).

If you want to try to send someone a test message, that's fine, but don't send a long message to do it. Very short is best—for instance, "This is a test; please let me know if it reached you."

- Your messages convey your persona—make sure you can stand behind them.

  Most people in the online world will know you only by what you say and how you say it. They may be your co-workers or friends someday. Take some time to make sure each message will not embarrass you later. Minimize your spelling errors, and make sure your article is easy to read and understand. Writing is an art, and doing it well requires practice. Since people on the net judge you largely on the basis of your writing, such time is well spent.

- Be professional and careful in what you say about others.

  E-mail is easily forwarded. If you hurt someone, however accidentally, that hurt can be magnified by the number of people the message gets sent to.

  To get even more specific about e-mail professionalism and courtesy, pay special heed to the next cybermanners rule:

- Nix Nixon: assume people don't want their information made public.

  It's considered poor cybermanners to let out any part of someone's personal information on the net when that person has not approved it. Such information includes any part of their e-mail messages, their e-mail address, or other personal information. Assume a person's information is *for your eyes only* if they do not specifically tell you otherwise. Ask for permission if you want to use it, such as quoting someone's e-mail in your own messages. Most netters will let you use it if you ask first.

One way to remember this pillar of cybermanners: "Nix Nixon"—that is, don't "pull a Nixon" by letting private matters become public. (Remember his infamous tapes? If not, watch the coverage of any recent scandal that involves a legal battle over diaries or private documents.)

In the Beginning: Message Headers

Headers contain those preliminary lines in an e-mail message, the stuff that comes before your actual text message. Examples are "From:" and "To:" (self-explanatory), "Cc:" (copies to send to other users, which can include yourself), and the "Subject:" line. Here's some advice for using these *fields* correctly.

▌ Snappy subjects snag attention; use descriptive titles.

The subject line of an article is there to enable a person with a limited amount of time to decide whether or not to read your article. The *subject header* is one of the most important components of an effective message. When a person receives dozens of electronic notes per day, a snappy and informative subject header will do a lot to put your message at the forefront.

Tell people what the article is about before they read it, in as specific a sentence as possible. A title like "Free O.J." is a bit general and vague—especially since it could be processed in multiple ways. Better would be "Supermarket Gives Away Orange Juice," or "Can the Trial of O.J. Simpson Be Free from Bias?"—depending on what your original intent was when you thought of using "Free O.J."

Don't expect people to read your article to find out what it is about; many of them won't bother.

Be especially careful of those e-mail packages that enter "none" by default in the subject header if you don't type one of your own. When it's the end of the day and a person is scanning their e-mail in-basket, the subject "none" is not likely to entice them into reading more. If the sender doesn't treat the message with some importance, why should the recipient?

- Focus on a single, concise subject per message.

The subject header is often the only means a person has of filing and retrieving messages in an intelligent way. This is why it is essential to send a separate message for each topic under discussion, each with its own distinct subject header. For example, sending a message entitled "Auto Accidents, Peanuts, and Bob Dole" is not good cybermanners, because you're placing the burden on the recipient to break up this message into three files if s/he needs to store the contents intelligently. Better cybermanners: send three messages, each with a unique title ("Auto Accidents," "Peanuts," and "Bob Dole").

You *could* think of each message as a novel or a report (but brief—remember the previous rule) with a unique title that sums up its content in the best manner. Remember those SAT questions where you had to devise titles for stories they provided? Well, now you get to use that college knowledge (if you're still repaying your student loans, maybe you'll feel better).

Also, keep subject titles brief; if they're too long, sometimes they can get cut off at the end. For example, some mail programs truncate the length of the subject line to 40 characters. Another good reason to avoid multiple-subject messages (since they'll tend to be longer).

One more note: you should avoid the "reply" command when you want to change the focus of discussion, and instead use the "send" command and a fresh subject header.

- Keep the list of recipients and *cc:s* ("carbon copies") to a minimum.

If you find yourself sending e-mail to the same group of people regularly (such as for a monthly newsletter), retyping all those addresses can get tiresome. Instead, most users can set up an *alias*—an e-mail address that represents several addresses that you specify. Just e-mail the alias, and all the addresses it represents will get the same piece of e-mail.

Another reason to use aliases on semi-public e-mail newsletters: some of the recipients may not want their e-mail address known to others. Using an alias keeps the address hidden (in your alias file). See the earlier rule on revealing people's information over e-mail.

If you've never heard of aliases before, don't fret; either consult a basic Internet technical book, or ask on the net. It's not crucial to use aliases, just more convenient.

■ Don't insult or criticize third parties without giving them a chance to respond.

For instance, leaving the third party's address out of the **Cc:** field of your message means they will not know of the insult or criticism, unless you or the other party *tells* the insultee, then you get into issues of talking behind that party's back, and so on. If you must express strong views about a third party, at least include that party in the ongoing dialog so they have the option of joining in or staying out of it.

The Middle: Message Size

Now we're getting to the heart of the matter. You've done your pre-writing pondering, and have that header stuff down pat. Time to write the text itself. Here are some rules to help you, focusing on the length of your messages. (You may've heard the cliché "Size doesn't matter"—that may be true in the real world, but not in cyberspace. So pay attention!)

■ Be brief.

Brevity is the soul of wit, and of good net messages. The ease of sending messages, among other factors, means it is easy for users to get up to hundreds of messages per day, hence being brief is a blessing to your reader. Increase the importance factor of this rule in proportion to how busy or prominent your reader is. (Did you know that Bill Gates, billionaire leader of Microsoft, spends five times as much time in e-mail as any other online activity? True! Stump your friends.)

Another benefit of brevity: succinct sentences result in greater impact on your reader. Also, a general rule of the net is that the number of people who'll be interested in reading a message is proportional to its length. Remember that it's more difficult to read long passages on a computer screen than on paper. The most effective e-mail messages shouldn't have to be printed out. One rationale for e-mail, after all, is saving on printing costs.

So take the time to be brief. Yes, you heard right. Paradoxically, it often takes more time to write shorter messages. Why? Because creative editing and idea distillation takes effort, and effort takes time.

▮ Go Goldilocks: not too short, not too long, but just right.

Given that you want to be brief in general, what is the proper size (that is, amount of content) for electronic messages?

A U-shaped utility curve seems to apply. Very terse short messages (like "Me too") with little content may make your reader irritated for having wasted his or her time. That is, they may experience a low "time-spent-to-knowledge-gained" ratio. Yet droning on and on may produce the same effect.

A good general rule: put as much information in as tight a space as possible; make it "info-dense." This rule becomes more relevant as the degree of importance of the message increases—for example, if it's business-related—and also depends on how time-limited your reader is. More casual, friendly messages need not be as strict in form. Bottom line: keep in mind the kind of person or group who will read your message, as well as their current state.

It's usually wise to adapt to your reader. For example, one of my professors in grad school always tended to send me short messages, and once commented that mine tended to be too long. You can guess how I adapted. I felt he was justified in his comments, since (being well known) he received a large amount of e-mail each day.

▮▮▮ Abbrev. when poss.

> Abbreviate whenever possible, that is. This relates to the previous two rules, but assumes your reader(s) know the abbreviations you are using. See the lists in Chapters 1 and 3 (as well as the Glossary) for useful abbreviations.

▮▮▮ Avoid irrelevancies.

> Yet another spinoff of the "brief" rule. However, if you feel absolutely compelled to include side comments, try putting them in an aside, labeling them as side comments. Or you can put them near the end, such as in a P.S.
>
> P.S. Aside: do you know the right way to label a second P.S.?
>
> P.P.S. That's right: it's P.P.S., short for "post post script." P.S.S. is incorrect (not to mention perilously close to taboo).

More Middle: General Message Content Rules

There's more to messages than their length, of course. The following rules go into even more detail about message text, covering both syntax (rhymes with "sin tax," for you political junkies) and semantic issues.

▮▮▮ Don't go overboard with abbrev's (avoid using if possible).

> While it's good to know what the customary abbreviations are, in case you get messages containing them, your message is likely to be clearer to your reader if you use as few as you can. Your reader may not know what they mean, and if your message gets forwarded, the odds of other readers not understanding your message increases.
>
> Here's a compromise: if you use the same word or phrase repeatedly over a long message (or over several messages), define an abbrev for each (at message beginning or end), and then feel free to use the abbrev. Now you've efficiently reduced the chances of *any* misunderstanding.

- Limit line length (60 characters max is best) and avoid special characters.

   In computer systems as well as romance, not everyone is compatible; assume your reader's system may be different from yours, and act accordingly. For example, some characters may look fine on your system, but could appear as garbage on your reader's screen. Some e-mail systems are more flexible than others when displaying text, but this rule will keep you safe.

   In addition, your system may allow more characters per line than your reader's, hence some lines might be cut off at the reader's end. Assume the worst and you can expect the best.

   Another reason to limit line length: lines of text that span the entire width of a wide screen are difficult to read. It is easier for the eye to follow short lines from one to the next. Finally, shorter line length helps when others forward or quote lines from your message, because forwarding and quoting programs often indent the included lines a bit.

   So, once again, make "brief" your mantra. Brief across the screen, brief down the screen, brief subject line, brief number of recipients, buy briefs on sale.

- Put carriage returns where they are needed.

   Many e-mail programs are like word processors; you can type an entire paragraph without pressing carriage return, because the programs will break lines automatically as they are displayed on your screen. Not all users, however, are so lucky. Try sending a test message addressed to yourself; if some of your text is missing on the right side, your messages are probably being truncated.

   If this is happening to you, don't type an entire paragraph or message in a single line; it looks sloppy, and is difficult to quote properly. Constant monitoring of your typing progress on the screen should help you avoid this, at least until you get used to inputting e-mail messages or get a new e-mail program. Several episodes of sending and analyzing test messages should help you figure out how to handle your mail typing properly.

Also, in many mail programs, it's not wise to put in a return after 81 or more columns, since on most systems this will show up as alternating long lines and really short lines.

Even if your system can handle reformatting messages so they look nice anyway, remember that many don't. If you aren't careful with inserting carriage returns, others will find your messages harder to read, and perhaps will even avoid reading your messages altogether.

- Don't use all caps, unless YOU YEARN TO YELL!

   Don't use all uppercase letters as your default text style. Such text is hard for the eye and brain to assimilate because it exhibits no contrast. In addition, using capital letters is interpreted by netters as shouting. If someone has stepped on your virtual toes, shouting may be appropriate. Otherwise, avoid it, unless you want to be mistaken for Morton Downey, Jr.

   Of course, like any rule, it can be bent a bit. It's OK to capitalize a few words to highlight an important point, or to distinguish a title or heading. *Asterisks* or _underscores_ surrounding a word also can be used to make a stronger point.

- All lowercase: almost always OK (but consider your reader).

   In e-mail communication, it is not mandatory to capitalize every sentence. This kind of informality is common in net mail, especially among friends. However, if you are writing a business-related message (such as responding to a job offer), you probably should use standard business-letter etiquette, such as caps when starting sentences.

Cybercommandments: Do's and Don'ts of E-mail Manners

- **Identify yourself and your affiliations clearly.**

  This is especially true in business communications, and helps the reader of your message understand where you are coming from, providing a context for your content.

- **Think about the level of formality you put in a message.**

  Thinking about your recipient helps here. When talking to a professor or President, you may wish to present a more formal tone. An e-mail to a loved one can, of course, have a lighter feel.

- **If you must express emotion in a message, label it clearly.**

  As mentioned earlier, it is harder to express emotion in e-mail than in most other media. Labeling emotional passages explicitly will ensure your intentions are understood correctly. In the middle of a heated reply to a colleague, for instance, someone might add a smiley to indicate a tongue-in-cheek remark, as in "Can't you see I'm always right? :)"

  Also, different people might interpret news in different ways. For instance, "Bill got the promotion :)" indicates a supporter of Bill; ending that sentence with :(obviously indicates a different reaction (e.g., the sadness of Bill's rival at the firm).

- **Be careful when using sarcasm and humor.**

  Without the voice inflections and body language of face-to-face personal communication, it's easy to misinterpret a remark meant to be funny. For example, what you intend as a joke may be viewed as criticism if your reader can't see your facial expression or hear your voice. Subtle humor tends to get lost, so make sure people realize you are trying to be funny. Using the various kinds of "smiley" emoticons can help here.

31

Be aware, however, that satire is frequently used in e-mail without any explicit indications. If a message outrages you, you should ask yourself whether it may just have been unmarked satire. Some puckish satirists bait the indignant by making outrageous statements with a well-crafted straight face, and several self-proclaimed connoisseurs of the art refuse to use smiley faces, so take heed or you may make a temporary fool of yourself.

This Is the End: Signatures and Final Checks

We're almost through these main Cybercommandments. The end of your message is also important, and—you guessed it—here's some more advice.

- At message's end, put a signature—preferably one that illustrates your personality.

    Your signature footer, or sig, is not required, but is an easy way to give others relevant info on you, without having to rewrite it repeatedly. Most netters have a signature added to their e-mail automatically by placing it in a special file (often called "$HOME/.signature," it may vary depending on your service provider).

    A standard sig would include your name, position, affiliation, and your Internet (e-mail) addresses. Every sig should at least include your return (e-mail) address; your system administrator can help you if you're not sure of its exact composition. Optional sig information can include your "real world" address and phone number (but exercise the same caution with these that you would in the real world). A nice benefit of sigs: when cleverly composed, they can show others your cyberstyle, and help readers understand where you (and your words) are coming from.

- Don't overdo signatures.

    Sigs are nice but, as with eating Oreos, don't overdo it. Sigs can tell the world something about you, but keep them short. A sig that is longer than the message itself is considered poor cybermanners. More than four or five lines is getting into poor-cybermanners territory.

Remember: the main purpose of a signature is to help people locate you on the net, not learn your life story.

▌ Prefer proofreading.

Another pitfall of e-mail is the degeneration of grammar and spelling due to the medium's split-second interactivity, and the temptation to reply off the top of the head. In the old days, secretarial staff and other colleagues often had a chance to catch the most blatant errors in memos and external correspondence. With e-mail, there's a tendency to avoid proofreading altogether. (Sometimes the effect on the language can be bizarre.)

Struggle against this tendency. Check spelling, punctuation, and grammar; save your fellow netters the unsoothing sensation of poor prose (unless you are e-mailing poetry, in which case all bets are off). Proofreading also helps make your message more readable, hence more likely to generate positive responses than those pesky flames from English-teacher-wanna-bes.

If you're lucky enough to have an e-mail package that includes a spelling checker, make it a habit (one of the few healthy habits we have left anymore, so why not take advantage).

▌ Assume that messages you send are permanent.

Remember: in cyberspace, if you do something wrong or in poor judgment, it can haunt you for a long time, and in many people's minds. Just pretend your e-mail is being displayed and dissected on The Tonight Show, and you'll be careful enough to check your message one last time.

But Wait, There's More: How to Respond Properly to Messages

You've read about e-mail construction techniques and (doubtless) heeded the sage advice offered here—now we must deal with *others'* messages.

- If you receive a message intended for another person, don't just ignore it.

  It is your duty to help get the message to the correct recipient—either by e-mailing the sender, or (if that fails) trying to forward the message to the proper receiver.

- Avoid responding while emotional.

  Emotions can spill over into your text and influence your words, to the point where you may regret the content you create.

- If a message generates emotions, look again.

  Could you be interpreting it incorrectly? Try to look for several possible meanings if you're not sure. You can always e-mail the sender for clarification, too.

- Assume the honesty and competence of the sender.

  In other words, give people the benefit of the doubt—especially if you know the person or their reputation (assuming it's a good one).

- Try to separate opinion from non-opinion while reading a message, so you can respond appropriately.

  If they have good cybermanners, they'll probably separate it for you. Or they may use emoticons to help guide your processing of their words.

  If there are no such cues for you, re-read the message several times, and come to clear conclusions about what you feel is opinion and what is not. Deal with each in an appropriate manner; opinion can certainly be argued with more easily than fact (unless, of course, you dispute what they called fact).

  So remember: one person's fact is another person's opinion. In general, you'll be a cool netter if you just follow Einstein's advice: it's all relative.

- Consider whom you should respond to.

Especially important if the message you received was problematic in some way—a flame. The last thing you want to do is compound someone's poor cybermanners with some of your own (which you would do if you respond with strong words to the wrong person or group).

Rules for More Specific E-mail Tasks

The rules we've just reviewed apply to all e-mail you send. Now I present assorted rules for other tasks you may face when composing some messages.

Giving Credit Where Credit Is Due

We all love to get credit, whether it's from MasterCard or from someone who liked our work. Here's how to give it properly.

- If you didn't write it, better cite it.

    Cite all quotes, references, and sources. If you are using facts to support a cause, state where they came from. Don't take someone else's ideas and use them as your own. You don't want someone pretending that your ideas are theirs; show the same respect to others (unless it's that Rodney D dude).

- Respect copyright and license agreements.

    Once something is sent out over the Internet, it is effectively in the public's reach. Note that e-mailing movie reviews, song lyrics, or anything else published under a copyright could cause you, your company, or the net itself to be held liable for damages, so operate with caution when using this material.

- When quoting another person, expend effort to edit!

    Take out whatever isn't directly applicable to your reply. Including an entire article will annoy those who read it. (More on proper quoting follows.)

Message Procreation: Forwarding, Copying, and Quoting

Rabbits and e-mail have something in common: both tend to proliferate profusely! Depending on your perspective, the widespread use in e-mail of message forwarding and cc:s ("carbon copies") can be benefit or bane. Forwarding e-mail to interested parties is the quickest way to get the right people involved in a decision or issue. On the other hand, in the business world, forwarding and carbon copying have a way of bypassing the traditional corporate structures, which might raise the eyebrows of management. (If you are unemployed or have dropped out of society, never mind.)

- Use message forwarding and carbon copying sparingly.

    Consider other options first. Rather than forwarding to someone all messages that relate to a topic, consider paraphrasing or quoting the relevant portions instead. This is less irritating for the reader than receiving a long and confusing conglomeration of messages, interspersed with the names, network addresses, times, dates, and general computer gibberish that e-mail programs love to append to every message.

    You're doing your e-mail correspondent a great favor by only bringing the relevant passages to their attention. And by the way: favors tend to be rewarded with return courtesy, so cybermanners spread, and before you know it everyone lives happily ever after! Well, at least online (and in those early Spielberg movies).

- Quote to be clear.

    One day, you or someone you know may perpetrate a heinous cybersin: sending a vague message like, "Could you send me that file again?" Well, what file is *that*, doofus? Especially if you've delayed responding to an electronic note for awhile, it's a good idea to forward, or selectively quote or paraphrase, the original correspondence so the recipient can clue in to the subject under discussion.

▥ Consider computer conferencing or mailing lists.

If you require a more interactive environment for electronic communication with multiple correspondents—that is, you crave a cooler cave to chill with your comrades—you can try other programs related to e-mail. For example, you could use a computer conferencing program (if your service provides one).

Or you can try a mailing list (see that kindly Kent chap's book *The Complete Idiot's Guide to the Internet* for more details). If you choose to get your words across via mailing lists, make sure you don't get into the junk-mail habit of broadcasting indiscriminately to lots of lists—which means lots of people will be getting your words.

Which can all be generalized into another cool jewel rule: *Give a hoot—don't e-pollute!*

Seeking Advice and Factual Information

Need help? Don't we all! Seriously, don't call Dear Abby, or Tommy Flanagan from Liars Anonymous, or even 411—and *definitely* not 911. Ask the net! But before you do:

Be selective in broadcasts for information!

Don't blanket the net in search of information. (Remember that classic beach film, *Search Blanket Wrongo*.) You may get an answer from one source and then a flood of duplicates from other sources, which wastes the latter folks' time (as well as yours when you have to delete all the duplicate e-mail).

Organizations' Considerations

Again, if you've sworn off the whole work-and-make-money thing, don't sweat these. By the way, *Roseanne*'s on.

▥ Follow chain-of-command procedures for corresponding with superiors.

For example, don't send a complaint via e-mail directly to the "top" just because you have the power to do so. It's a pain in the butt to rewrite your sig file after you lose that posh work address (or so I've been told).

- Don't use one type of network for another type of work.

For instance, you wouldn't want to use an academic network for commercial or proprietary work. Or turn your ivory tower into The Watchtower (that's an oblique religious reference—meant to convey that, for example, it's poor cybermanners to over-evangelize on a network when access has been given unto thee for free).

- Use discretion when forwarding mail to group addresses or distribution lists.

One of the goals here is to limit redundancy on the net. Granted, sending lots of copies of the same long file does not cost any trees, as paper copies would, but the time uninterested readers have to spend scanning and deleting such files does add up. For example, it is preferable to reference the source of a document and provide instructions on how to obtain a copy.

Congratulations! You've made it through the main rules for e-mail manners. Hopefully this very complete collection—arguably the most thorough in print to date—will answer most of the common questions you may have, and keep your electronic-message habits in great shape for some time. This is, of course, IMHUO (in my humble unbiased opinion).

How to Learn More About E-mail Manners

Of course, there *is* a small statistical probability that one of your questions may not be answered somewhere in these pages. To help address this possibility, you'll find some meta-rules-of-thumb (rules for finding rules) in these humble paragraphs.

And if you *do* discover some new rules for cybermanners that you or others feel strongly about, feel free to forward them to me at my (what else?) e-mail address.

They may make it into future editions of this book! (Or, at the very least, they'll make amusing anecdotes when I plug this book on the talk show circuit.)

When you need an answer about net-related manners, try the net itself. Many resources exist around the net that deal with cybermanners. After reading this book, if you still have questions, check the net before doing anything else, and see if your answer awaits there.

For example, you could use online search tools like Gopher and Archie (no, I'm not coming down with cute-itis, those are real program names) to search for files based on keywords you type in—such as **manners** or **etiquette**. Some of the rules listed here were inspired by, or adapted from, information found using such search methods. Also note that some commercial online services, such as PRODIGY, provide their own manners guides.

If the Net Can't Answer Your Questions, Ask Another Netter

You'd be surprised how many helpful folks are out there in the virtual village. ("I never met a netter I didn't like," to quote CyberWill Rogers.) If you have a question related to proper cybermanners and cannot find an answer in this book or in some net-based source, a short e-mail message to a friend, colleague, or service department of an online service can often (ahem) net you an answer.

Summary Points

To close this chapter, here is a quick recap of the general rules of e-mail manners.

- Remember that the person on the other side is human, and target the right audience.
- Be professional and careful in what you say about others, and assume people don't want their info made public.

- Snappy subjects snag attention; use descriptive titles, and focus on a single concise subject per message.
- Don't use all caps, unless YOU YEARN TO YELL!
- If you must express emotion in a message, clearly label it, and be careful when using sarcasm and humor.
- Avoid responding while emotional.

chapter 3

Using USENET and Virtual Global Bulletin Boards

In This Chapter

The first two chapters dealt only with the domain of electronic mail communication. We now change focus to a related arena: communications via electronic bulletin boards, or *bboards*.

In this section, you'll read about:

- The basics of what bboard systems like USENET are.
- How to compose a standard bboard message.
- The most commonly used embellishments to basic bboard messages (in other words, more useful cyberese).

What Are Virtual Bulletin Boards and the Ubiquitous USENET?

The biggest collection of bboards on the Internet is known as USENET—a kind of global "network of bboards" that are grouped into a huge number of topics, ranging from the simple to the complex, from arcane subjects to current events. (As mentioned earlier in the book, USENET bboards are usually called "newsgroups" on the net, but I use the term "bboard" to refer to any bulletin board on USENET *or related services*—such as CompuServe, America Online, PRODIGY, or other smaller online services.)

Composed of as many as a million messages at any given time, USENET is akin to e-mail because it enables people from around the globe to communicate. However, unlike e-mail, bboards allow anyone with access to them to read their messages—very much like real bulletin boards.

In fact, to best visualize USENET, you can first picture a regular old bulletin board. You can stick notes on it. Now picture it hanging up at a public space, like at work by the water cooler. Anyone can stick notes on that bboard, and anyone can come by and read the notes. Of course, the virtual board's "surface" is, in a sense, as tall and wide as the planet; hence, many feel bboard manners are even more important to learn and apply than those for e-mail, since many more eyes will see any errors you make.

Now picture thousands of bboards existing in an electronic space, and that's the essence of what USENET is. Each bboard in USENET has a name composed of several words separated from each other by periods, for example, "soc.singles" and "comp.ai."

Note that other non-Internet and commercial services—such as PRODIGY, CompuServe, and America Online—also have bboard systems, usually referred to as "forums." Nearly all the rules and facts that follow apply to them as well, but I will assume the USENET when I discuss bboards in this chapter.

How to Compose a Standard Bboard Message

Since you've already read the section on composing e-mail messages, you are 99% of the way there already! A bboard message is, at first glance, the same as an e-mail message;

they can have the same content. (Whether it is good cybermanners to *have* such similar content is a different issue—to be dealt with later.) Instead of sending to a person or persons, a *bboard post* is a message you send to a bulletin board that exists only in the cyberspace of the net. Again, you can (in theory) put anything in a bboard post that you can in an e-mail message.

For more detail on composing and posting bboard messages, read (you guessed it) one of the more nuts-and-bolts Internet basics books (like Mr. Kent's).

Embellishments: Some Bboard Cyberese

In Chapter 1 we saw examples of abbreviations, words, and phrases used on the net; although I discussed them in relation to e-mail, they apply to bboard messaging as well.

Some newsgroups on the net, however, develop their own cyberese; often they are common in messages sent within that group's members, but not used as much outside that *mailing circle*. For example, here's a sampling of abbreviations recommended by the "soc.singles" newsgroup on USENET:

MOTOS	Member Of The Opposite Sex
MOTSS	Member Of The Same Sex
MOTAS	Member Of The Appropriate Sex
MOTIS	Member Of The Inappropriate Sex
SO	Significant Other
RP	Romantic Partner
POSSLQ	Person of Opposite Sex Sharing Living Quarters
LO	Lust Object (occasionally also Love Object)
RI	Romantic Interest
POW	Problem Older Woman

Chapter 3

PYM	Problem Younger Man (also ProblemYounger Mutant)
POM	Problem Older Man
PYW	Problem Younger Woman
NG	Nice Guy/Gal
SNAG	Sensitive New-Age Guy
LJBF	Let's Just Be Friends (now considered a verb)
PDA	Public Display of Affection
LDR	Long Distance Relationship
LTR	Long-Term Relationship
SMV	Sexual Market Value
LAFS	Love At First Sight (or "Love At First Site" for those in a hurry)
TL&EH	True Love & Eternal Happiness
NIFOC	Nude In Front Of Computer
FOAF	Friend Of A Friend

And, of course, who can do without:

WFYITBWNBLJO	Waiting For You In The Bathtub Wearing Nothing But Lime Jell-O

Probably the longest abbreviation you've ever seen (it was for me). It needs its *own* abbreviation.

Note that just because "soc.singles" discusses these abbreviations, and its readers may be the ones using these abbreviations the most, that doesn't mean they can't be used by anyone. However, it is good manners to consider your reader before using one of these—or any abbreviation or cyber-related buzzword—since s/he may not know the meaning.

Also note that there is no rule forcing you to use any of these abbreviations, or any specialized words/phrases. On the other hand, if you regularly read or post to "soc.singles" and do *not* understand the abbreviations listed here, you may find that you don't understand some of the posts.

The bottom line: be hip to who you are communicating with. If it's a USENET newsgroup or other kind of bboard, find out if there are special rules, abbreviations or cyberese associated with that group (to learn where to look, read on). If there are, try your best to follow or use them.

Get the Meaning

You may run across some words and phrases on the USENET that are unclear to you. Here's a partial list of these words and their meanings.

Bulletin board, or **bboard**   Although several meanings exist in the computer world, I use this term to represent the virtual space to which netters send messages for other netters to read and respond to. So named because the virtual space exhibits the features of real-world bulletin boards: multiple people can post notes on them, and just as many people can stop by and read them.

Newsgroup   The USENET term for what I call a *bboard*. Note that they don't all contain news—in fact, opinions probably outweigh fact on the majority of newsgroups.

Newsreader   Program that you use to read bboard (such as USENET) posts.

FAQ   Frequently Asked Question(s). Often refers to the FAQ of a particular bboard. Most bboards have FAQs so that endlessly repeated questions do not clog the net; newbies can just look up the answer in the FAQ. One can also find specialized rules and cyberese here.

FAQs are usually posted as a bboard message periodically (every few weeks); the FAQ for bboard X would be posted on bboard X itself. Some FAQs are also stored in databases that can be viewed or downloaded by using special Internet programs (see Mr. Kent's book for more details).

Bandwidth   The virtual size of the virtual lanes of the net "highway." Not really a defined word; more of a metaphor for net activities. Often used in a problem sense, as in "you're using up valuable bandwidth with your irrelevant flame—get a life!" What is clogged when too many FAQ-resident questions still get asked anyway.

USENETizen   A citizen (or denizen, if you prefer "d" words) of the USENET-bboard cyberverse. Or, if you prefer less flash, one who uses USENET.

Flamebait   A cousin of the already-defined word "flame." Something posted publicly that appears designed to inspire flames; usually this is a post that is not only likely to annoy a lot of people, but is also worded in such a way as to arouse the ire of readers. Some sure-fire species of flame bait:

"Why don't you just keep your big yap shut?"

"I hate the Mac. Anyone care to argue this point?"

"I'm lookin' for some action. Anyone interested? Signed, Horny."

"I haven't read the FAQ yet—I thought I'd save some time by asking the net first. Here's my question ..."

Posting any of the following *without* any context given: "Yep."; "Me too."; "OK."; "Sure."

Dictionary flame   A post that corrects someone's definition or use of a word. Sometimes the flamer's initial intentions are good—to help someone learn—but this person's "teacher" side gets carried away with language and tone (e.g., becomes condescending). Magnify the flame's "damage" if the flamer sent THE BBOARD his/her flame, and not just the original erroneous netter. The vast majority of bboard readers don't care about this error, and you can imagine the embarrassment felt by the original netter who was flamed. Hence flaming on a bboard can easily start a flame war.

Spelling flame   Related to dictionary flame; a post correcting a previous article's spelling in a showy fashion as a sneaky means of belittling or undermining the article's content, instead of actually responding to that content. Ironic note: spelling flames often contain their own errors in speling (oops! don't flame me). Another note: netters who are usually sloppy spellers may be more sensitive to this issue, and hence might interpret *any* correction as a spelling flame. Similar concerns and consequences as for dictionary flames.

Lurker   Users who read bboard groups but never post to them. The behavior itself is referred to as "lurking."

GIF, or .GIF   This abbreviation stands for "Graphics Interchange Format" and is a common format in which pictures are stored for display on a computer screen. When discussions turn visual, some netters might offhandedly ask for a "GIF file"—meaning they want a picture—but even if you're asked for one, it is generally considered poor cybermanners to post GIF files to newsgroups because they tend to be quite large in size.

post   (noun) The message you sent to the bboard. (verb) To send the message.

posting   Sending a message to a bboard.

crossposting   Sending the same message to multiple bboards.

editing   A term often used to discuss the practice of *deleting unnecessary quoted material* from your messages. Being another essential element for ensuring good message quality, however, editing naturally applies to all areas of a message, not just quotes. It's good cybermanners to take the time to edit your message down to maximum brevity, while still making your point clearly.

killfiles No, it's not the name of the new James Bond thriller. Many newsreaders provided by online services have a provision for "killing" messages; that is, marking them as read before you get to them, so your newsreader then skips over them automatically instead of showing them to you. Kill commands may be placed in a file where they will be performed automatically when you read a group. Some systems let you not only kill the topic you're reading, but also kill that topic in future sessions.

However, keep in mind that most topics die or change over time, and unless you edit that line out of your killfile, it will continue to live in there, eating up processor time and generally slowing everything down whenever you read that group.

In general, it is good cybermanners to keep your killfiles to a minimum , especially if you are sharing a computer with other users who don't like the system bogging down any more than you do.

Summary Points

- Bboard messages are essentially like e-mail messages.
- Most of the assumptions and conventions learned for e-mail can transfer smoothly to the bboard domain.
- Some bboards carry their own specialized cyberese. Learning these new words, phrases, and abbreviations will make it easier for you to understand others' posts, and minimize the chance of misunderstandings.
- When misunderstandings do arise, flames can occur—messages that, for instance, represent someone's "hot" temper in words. If you or others flame back, flame wars can break out, which wastes net bandwidth and generally bogs down the net.

chapter 4

Cybercommandments II: Do's and Don'ts of Bboard Manners

In This Chapter

- Why you need good bboard manners
- General rules for bboard manners
- How to learn more about bboard manners
- Q & A on bboard manners

Why You Need Good Bboard Manners

Pretty much the same reasons you need good e-mail manners. Now multiply the importance by the number of people who can read your bboard message (your post) around the world—millions! So one could argue that manners are even more important for bboard messages—and, of course, I have many tips to help improve your cybermanners in this new arena.

Remember, a post to a bboard is essentially the same in structure and content as an e-mail message, so many of the same rules apply. In fact, in general, you can assume this is the case.

Some General Rules of Thumb for Bboard Manners

Now here are some rules most relevant to electronic bulletin boards. The information, like that contained in the earlier e-mail rules, has been culled from various sources, including the net itself, and represents a distillation and generalization of the best advice found.

Some Things Are Better Left Unsaid: What Not to Post

Here's a few pointers on things that are not cool to post onto USENET.

- Avoid posting messages of a personal nature. In other words, never send private messages to a public "virtual hangout," which a bulletin board is. Use e-mail instead. Not only will the message recipient be grateful, but so will bboard users who don't care about your personal message anyway.

- Avoid posting messages of an emotional nature.

    Emotional issues should be "put in their place"—special newsgroups that have been created just for them. Topics like abortion, politics, religion, and other such things are best avoided in regular bboards, not because they aren't important issues to discuss, but because such "hot topics" can easily take over a newsgroup, and drive off those who participate on group X because they love talking about (what else) topic X. Anyone who wants to debate abortion can go to talk.abortion, and anyone who wants to post and read personals can go to alt.personals*—but if newsgroup xyz gets turned into xyz.personals.abortion.religion.politics, there's no newsgroup where the xyz people can go to continue their discussions.

- Avoid posts that are void and devoid of real content.

    Avoid messages that are pretty much content-free: don't, for example, quote an entire message that you agree with and then append "Yeah, what she said" to the end. Test messages should also be avoided—if you're unsure whether your messages are getting out or not, post something to misc.test and you'll get confirmation messages from various sites around the world to let you know your posting software is working.

■ Don't post others' e-mail without permission.

A big USENET no-no. In the interests of privacy, it's considered extremely bad taste to post any e-mail that someone may have sent, unless they explicitly give you permission to redistribute it. While the legal issues can be heavily debated, most everyone agrees that e-mail should be treated as anything one would receive via normal snail-mail, complete with all the assumed rights that are carried with it.

■ Avoid "what-computer-is-best" debates.

Everyone's got an opinion about which computer hardware or software is best. No matter what kind of computer a person is using, theirs is *always* the best and most efficient of them all. Simply asking innocently which system is best can generate a flood of mail—some polite, some flame, but all waste, especially since the arguments have all been hashed out time and time again. For instance, posting articles asking questions like "What computer should I buy? An IBM-compatible or a Mac?" will lead only to fervent arguments over the merits and drawbacks of each brand.

The best cybermanners in such a case is to bypass the net entirely; instead, visit a local user group, or do some research of your own (like reading some magazine reviews). Remember: don't e-pollute the net-waves!

■ Avoid and ignore "dying child" posts; choose charities.

Dying is terrible. Dying children even sadder. But when a post appears asking for a world-record number of letters to be sent to the child, so s/he can get into Guiness's famous book, all sources of USENET manners say it's to be ignored. Instead, try sending the postage you'd save to

51

a valid charity; you'll help at least one child this way, and be sure you are doing so. The postage you'd waste sending letters does not help any child.

- Cast a chink in chain letters: avoid 'em and ignore 'em.

Another example of how we clever humans love to imitate—taking the worst of our real society and mimicking it in the cyberverse as well. If you know someone who's actually made a mint from a chain letter, real or virtual, e-mail me and I'll eat my hat, as soon as I buy one. Once again, note that in some cases, posting these types of messages can result in your account being revoked.

- Avoid posts about recent news.

One should avoid posting "recent" events—sports scores, a plane crash, or anything people can see on the evening news or read in the morning paper. News is often old by the time your post is broadcast on the bboards—especially when your post is a response to an older one. By the time the article has propagated across all of USENET, the "news" value of the article will have become stale. (This is one case for the argument that "USENET news" is a misnomer.)

Of course, there *are* exceptions—for instance, events like the 1991 Soviet coup. Computer networks were instrumental in getting the news of it out despite attempted blackouts. One way to determine such exceptions is to monitor how much message volume is appearing on a given topic; if it's high, then it's probably considered "real news," in which case it's okay to post on this topic.

- Avoid the urge to flame minor errors.

Spelling and/or grammar flame wars generally begin when someone posts an article correcting the spelling or grammar in some article. The immediate result seems to be for everyone on the net to turn into an English teacher and pick apart each other's postings for a few weeks.

If you catch a spelling error or a typo or an incorrect definition—or anything you consider an error—in someone else's post, think about whether it is a minor mistake and should be ignored or an important error that should be brought to everyone's attention. It does very little good to post a public message about minor errors, since the other readers will either have noticed the error themselves—and don't need to be told about it—or they won't care—in which case they don't need to be told about it. This behavior can also make people who used to be friends angry with each other.

If it's an informational post that's going to be reposted later, or a signature, you may want to inform the poster—in e-mail *only*. But if you can't turn the spelling error into an outrageously witty observation (like if the original poster has just made a screamingly funny Freudian slip in print), there's no reason to post these types of flames publicly. Remember that we all make mistakes, and that many users on the net use English as a second language. For that matter, there may be a typo. Not all netters are brilliant typists. If you feel you must comment on the quality of a posting, please do so by mail, not on the network.

Finally, remember this: there's so much incredible stuff on the net that you'll never get to all of it in your lifetime—why waste time on nonproductive flames?

- If you cannot resist adding to a "pun chain," don't quote all the puns so far and then add a pun that already appears earlier in the message.

If you do think of a pun or other witty rejoinder to add to someone else's article, it's a good idea to read any follow-ups that have already been posted before posting your witty response, just to make sure that three or four people haven't made the same remark already.

Finding the Right Bboard to Post To

- To find relevant bboards for your post, try searching before asking.

Unlike the real world, where in most cases asking directions is best (to save time and gas driving around aimlessly), the net lets you navigate without wasting any gas—and answers to your questions may lie in many places on the net.

To find what groups are relevant for your subject, you might scan through your local list of available newsgroups to see which group names seem related. (This is easy to do if your bboards are structured hierarchically; if not, you can always ask your online service's system administrator.) Then subscribe to those groups, and look at some of the recent traffic to make sure your question is suitable for the group. For example, job-seekers should post résumés to "misc.jobs.resumes," not "misc.jobs.offered."

- If you are still uncertain as to what groups are the best venue for your post, ask in news.groups.questions.

  You can do this after you have checked local resources, and the formal newsgroup descriptions. This group is designed for people to ask what existing newsgroup is appropriate for a given topic or sub-topic of discussion.

- If your site does not carry the newsgroup(s) where your post belongs, do *not* post it in other inappropriate groups.

  It's tempting, but resist. Very few sites carry all available newsgroups; for one thing, there are thousands of them. Your local news administrator can help you access newsgroups that are not currently available, or explain why certain groups are not available at your site.

- Test only on true testing grounds.

  Many people, particularly newbies, want to try out posting before actually taking part in discussions. The mechanics of getting messages out is often the most difficult part of using USENET. To this end, many users find it necessary to post their tests to "normal" groups (for example, misc.misc). This is a triple-M (major manners mistake) in the USENET arena. Messages in misc.misc that say "This is a test" are likely to cause large numbers of flaming hot messages to stream your way. If you want to try a test of something—and you should, particularly if you're a newbie—do not use a normal newsgroups as your testing ground. (This is especially true if the group is global!)

Several groups, called *test groups*, exist solely for the purpose of trying out a news system, reader, or even a new signature. Your system administrator can tell you what they are. Some places you might use include misc.test and alt.test. Some of the testing bboards will generate replies to your messages to inform you that they made it through. There are certain USENETizens that frequent the test groups to help new users out. They respond to the posts, often including the article so the poster can see how it got to the person's site. Also, many local/regional hierarchies have test groups.

You've Got the Right Newsgroup. Now, Before You Post ...

▌ Lurk before you leap!

When in doubt, read the newsgroup for a while, at least until you get a feel for what's going on. Perhaps the easiest way to learn how to use USENET is to watch how others use it. Start reading the news and try to figure out what people are doing and why. After a couple of weeks you will start understanding why certain things are done and what things shouldn't be done.

You may feel more at ease jumping into a conversation in progress than initiating your own. Don't feel shy about "butting in": one of the advantages of the net is that everyone can get a word in without interrupting anyone else or being thought rude for speaking up. Keep reading until you get to a message that inspires an interesting comment or observation of your own, and put that in a follow-up message. If you're feeling really brave, start a whole new thread—invite others' comments on a subject you think is interesting.

- Target the right audience.

  When you post an article, think about the people you are trying to reach. Asking computer-related questions on a newsgroup dealing with autos will not reach as many of the people you want to reach as if you asked them on the computer-related bboards. Try to get the most *appropriate* audience for your message, not the *widest*.

Ensuring Message Tone and Quality

Newsgroups are read by millions worldwide, most of whom base their impressions of you as a person entirely on the messages you post. Hence, it's worthwhile to make sure your messages are clear and readable, and convey the tone you intend.

- Pay attention to what you say—it *makes* you who you are on the net.

  How you write and present yourself in your articles is important. If you have terrible spelling, keep a dictionary nearby. If you have trouble with grammar and punctuation, try to get a book on English grammar and composition (found in many bookstores and garage sales). For an unstuffy-but-no-nonsense grammar source, I recommend Sheridan Baker's *The Practical Stylist*, which has been around in college composition courses for years; you should be able to find a used copy in any campus bookstore.

- Be clear. Muddy or excessively detailed posts are no-no's, Nanette.

  Ambiguous or vague questions often lead to no response at all, leaving the poster discouraged. Give as much essential information as you feel is necessary to let people help you, but keep it within limits.

- Error × attitude = flammability (flame factor, that is).

  Your potential for generating a flame response in others often goes up if you pick on a newbie (often preceded by "poor defenseless"), or pick on someone *when you yourself are in error* about what you are saying. Picking on errors when you act with an attitude multiplies the "flammability" of your message.

Word your messages carefully; this also affects the flame potential of your message. Since computers can't portray the inflection or tone in a person's voice, how articles are worded can directly affect the response to them.

If you say, "Anyone who wears plaid pants should jump off a cliff," you'll definitely get some responses—probably with the same advice. Rather than being inflammatory, phrase your article in a way that expresses your opinion rationally, like, "Is there a proper place for plaid in today's fashion?" Such an approach presents you as a much more level-headed individual. To reinforce this impression, follow another cardinal rule from the e-mail section: don't use all caps, or you will seem to be SHOUTING. In general, write as you would in a letter to a friend, following the normal rules of your language.

I Like It on Top: Choosing Good Subject Header Lines

▮▮ Be specific, yet not overly wordy, in subject lines.

Many people scan the "Subject:" lines of newsgroups, and choose to read only articles with subject lines that interest them. If your subject line does not contain useful information about the contents of your post, relatively few people will read it.

For instance: you are more likely to get useful replies with a subject of "Need file conversion utility from Microsoft Word to ACME-Write Pro" than with a subject of "Help!" On the flip side, overly wordy "Subject:" lines can be irritating. More examples:

Good:

Subject: Can't start my '89 Ford Escort on cold mornings

Subject: Want to locate Dr. Hoffenfeffer in D.C.

Bad:

Subject: I can't get my car to work!!!

Subject: I am most desperately in search of the honorable Dr. Hoffenfeffer in the city of

Note that the last example was cut off; too long a subject line can lead to this happening. Strive to keep your subjects to under 60 characters as a general rule; find out the *maximum* by checking around on your local online service, or sending test messages to yourself with different subject lengths. Remember, think of what will best help the reader when s/he encounters your article in a newsreading session.

- Know which newsgroups have a "standard" for subject-line format and content.

For example, postings in misc.jobs.offered are expected to contain the job title and location in the subject line, and postings in rec.games.board are expected to list the name of the specific game. It is always a good idea to scan the contents of a newsgroup to see if there is a common format in use. Also, read the FAQ for that group (that is, consult the list of Frequently Asked Questions that frequently gets posted on most bboards).

If you are following up another post, make sure the subject is relevant to your post (and vice versa). If you change the topic away from the original one, you should probably change the subject line, too.

The Meat of the Matter: Content Issues

- Separate opinion from non-opinion, and clearly label each.

Personally, I take whatever people say with a grain of salt—that is, unless a passage is labelled as fact, I assume that everything is someone's opinion (and opinions even vary about what constitutes a "fact"). But that's when I read. When I send, I want to be clear when something is fact or close to it (such as, "The SL-9 comet is going to crash into Jupiter today"), and when something is someone's opinion (such as, "Some astronomers predict the comet crash will lead to the extinction of all life on Earth. Not a minute too soon").

Another point: looking at the just-cited opinion about the comet, one would probably assume that the "not a minute too soon" comment was not made by the astronomers, but rather by the person who sent the message. Still, in the absence of clear labelling, one of the astronomers could (in theory) try to sue the sender for slander. So don't take chances; when in doubt, label clearly.

Another reason to separate opinion from non-opinion: to avoid flames. If you say some strong words but make it clear it is IYHO (in your humble opinion), others are more likely to give you a break. If you talk as if your word is gospel, and have a superior attitude to boot, you are increasing the odds of tons (OK, virtual tons) of opinionated e-mail coming your way. Decide if you really want that to happen! (The online service you use may not like all the tonnage either, since volumes of hate e-mail can clog or even crash it!)

▌ When content is questionable, encrypt it.

Certain newsgroups have messages in them that may be offensive to some people. (The rec.humor bboard is one example; we already discussed how humor is easily misinterpreted, often with undesirable consequences.) One way to ensure that such messages are not read unless explicitly requested is to encrypt them—that is, "scramble" messages so the content looks like garbage to the "naked" eye but actually has hidden meaning. One standard encryption method on the net is to rotate each letter by thirteen characters so that an "a" becomes an "n"; decryption then uncovers the hidden meaning by "unrotating" the letters by the same amount of the original rotation. This is known on the network as "rot13" (rot being shorthand for rotate) and when you rotate a message the word "rot13" should be in the "Subject:" line. Note that any number, not just 13, would serve the purpose here.

In fact, for even more encryption (if you're a paranoid nerd), you could always randomly select the number of rotations each time you encrypt something. Of course, you should ask yourself if your average message is worth all this!

Some software programs used to read USENET articles have a way of encrypting and decrypting messages (unless you're an immortal, encryption/decryption by hand just takes way too long). Your system administrator can tell you how the software on your system works.

■ Summarize what you are following up.

When you are following up someone's article, most netters expect you to summarize the parts of the article to which you are responding. This allows readers to appreciate your comments, rather than trying to remember what the original article said. (To get the economist part of your brain in on this, imagine the comparison between the extra time you spend summarizing and the amount of time spent by others in understanding your message's roots; the latter savings will nearly always be far greater than your time investment.) Another reason to include summaries of previous messages: it's possible for your response to get to some sites before the original article does! (Yes, pseudo-timewarps *are* possible in the brave new world of the Internet.)

Most netters feel that summarizing is best done by including appropriate quotes from the original article. Do not include the entire article because it will irritate the people who have already seen it. Even if you are responding to the entire article, summarize only the major points you are discussing.

■ Honor requests for "e-mail only" replies.

Authors of articles occasionally say that readers should reply by mail and they'll summarize. Accordingly, readers should do just that—reply via mail. Responding with a follow-up article to such an article defeats the intention of the author. S/he will eventually post one article containing the highlights of the responses she received. If you send a follow-up to the whole group, the author may not read what you have to say.

Even if you are not explicitly asked to send e-mail in lieu of a bboard post, do it anyway. One reason to do it this way is practical: a big problem on the net is that when someone asks a question, many people send out identical answers. When this happens, dozens of identical answers pour through the net. If instead you mail your answer to the person and suggest they summarize to the network, the net will only see a single copy of the answers, no matter how many people answer the question.

So do your part; if you post a question to the net, please remind people to send you the answers by mail, and offer to summarize them to the network.

▍ Honor requests for anonymity.

Sometimes people will respond to your post via e-mail, but request to remain anonymous (one example is the employees of a corporation that feel the information's not proprietary, but at the same time want to protect themselves from in-house political backlash). Summaries should honor this request accordingly by listing the "From:" address as "anonymous" or "(Address withheld by request)."

▍ When summarizing, *summarize*.

When you request information from the net, it is common courtesy to report your findings so that others can also benefit. When creating a summary of the replies to a post, it is also helpful to make it as reader-friendly as possible. For example, you should avoid simple dumping of all messages received into one big file.

Instead, it is good cybermanners to take some time and edit the messages into a form that contains the essential information other readers would be interested in. The best way of doing this is to take all the responses you received and edit them into a single article that is posted to the places where you originally posted your question. Take the time to delete *headers* (that is, the cyberese stuff that precedes the actual content of a message, such as Subject:, To:, and From: fields). Also, combine duplicate information and write a short summary. Try to credit the information to the people who sent it to you, where possible.

- Read all follow-ups and don't repeat what has already been said.

    Before you submit a follow-up to a message, read the rest of the messages in the newsgroup to see whether someone has already said what you want to say. If someone has, don't repeat it.

- Label or encrypt answers and spoilers.

    When you post something (like a movie review that discusses a detail of the plot) which might spoil a surprise for other people, please mark your message with a warning so that they can skip the message. Another alternative would be to use encryption methods to mask the message so it cannot be read accidentally. When you post a message with a spoiler, it's good cybermanners to include the word "spoiler" as part of the "Subject:" line.

Quoting Others' Messages

When following up on an article, many newsreaders provide a facility that lets netters quote the original article with each line prefixed by a special character. For instance:

> In article <789@ACME.net>, neil-armstrong@tranquility.base.com wrote:

> > I loved Forrest Gump, especially the haircuts. Buzz is the buzz now.

> > I wonder how Buzz Aldrin feels. Buzz cuts have definitely landed!

What kind of rules apply to quoting? Glad you asked.

- Delete quoted text from the original message if it isn't necessary to what you're trying to say ...

    It's not at all unusual for newbies to reply to long messages by quoting the entire thing, and then responding to a comment made somewhere in the middle of the original post by adding a single sentence at the end. Instead, when you quote another person, edit out whatever isn't directly applicable to your reply—being careful not to change their words (or it wouldn't be a *quote* anymore, now would it?)—and quote as little of previous messages as possible to make your point without distorting by omission. This gives the reader of the new article a better idea of what points you were addressing. If you include the entire article, you'll only annoy those reading it.

It may help to remind yourself that many people out there in Netland, when they see huge reams of quoted material that sadly lack editing, will simply skip over to the next message without bothering to read your sterling prose at the end. A little attention to the mechanisms of cleaning up quoted material will help you get your points across.

- … but leave enough quoted text so that readers will know the gist of what you're discussing.

  Even if they don't remember the message you're responding to, they should be able to get the gist of it in your summary. In other words, don't be *overly* industrious when deleting text.

- Avoid being tedious with responses.

  Instead of picking apart an article, address it in parts or as a whole. Addressing nearly every word of a post hints that the person responding has nothing better to do with the precious gift of time they have left on this dear sacred much-maligned planet (oops—my flame muscles are getting worked up for the next chapter).

- If a "war" starts—where insults and personal comments get thrown back and forth—take it outside!

  That is, take it to e-mail. Exchange personal messages with the person you're arguing with. No one enjoys watching people bicker incessantly; we can always watch reruns of *Moonlighting* if we want that.

- Don't trim off the attributions (the names of the people saying the things you're quoting) that go with the text you leave in.

  Do, however, remove the names of people whose comments have been entirely deleted.

- Signatures in the original quoted message aren't necessary.

   The readers already know who wrote it by the "attribution" line above the quote.

- More quotation may be necessary as the time between the original and your response increases.

   This is common sense; as memory fades, we need more reminders. In addition, new readers to this topic thread may have never seen the original posts (or older reminders) at all.

- Delete any quoted material left at the end of your message.

   It's easy to respond to something in the middle or even the beginning and forget to lop off the quoted stuff at the end that you aren't responding to.

This the End, My Friend: How to Finish a Post

- Follow the same signature rules as in the e-mail chapter ...

- ... but remember that millions may be reading your sig.

   Which means putting ads in your sig may be tempting. A commercial sig, however, will usually get you flamed. At which point you'll probably take it out.

- And *don't* re-post the article just to include the sig.

   The content is the crux; sigs only complement it at best. The gain in adding the sig info is usually outweighed by USENETters' anger over the wasted bandwidth (i.e., the using up of info-highway capacity by your duplicate message).

Crossposting (and Switching) to New Bboards

- Look both ways before you cross(post) the (info)highway.

   Avoid *crossposting* (posting a message to more than one bboard) unless you are sure it's appropriate. If you feel you must, limit yourself to no more than three or four.

For example, it is nearly always considered bad form to post to groups that are mostly unrelated, like sending a message to both "misc.invest" and "misc.jobs.offered." If it belongs in one newsgroup, it probably does not belong in the other.

If you do post to multiple newsgroups, do not post to each group separately. Instead, specify all the groups on a single copy of the message. This reduces network overhead, and lets people who subscribe to more than one of those groups see the message *once* instead of having to wade through each copy.

▌ Go for relevance, not reach.

Think very carefully before crossposting to more than one, or even two, newsgroups. It is considered highly inappropriate to broadcast your message to a wide selection of newsgroups merely to have more people read it. Instead, think of how relevant a bboard is to your message. Remember that many people automatically ignore articles posted to more than two or three groups. Also, read the FAQ for a newsgroup—and do some lurking—before you crosspost to that group.

When in doubt, peruse the rules of USENET etiquette listed in the bboard "news.announce.newusers"; other bboards also carry useful rules.

▌ Keep track of message evolution, and change bboards as needed.

Often, even when an article is appropriate for multiple newsgroups, it *is* desirable to redirect all follow-up discussion into one particular newsgroup. For instance, in the course of bboard dialog, the original subject may no longer be relevant or fully accurate to later messages. For example, a message on dogs may evolve into a discussion of wolves, then werewolves, then horror films. One must recognize when a dialog has changed to the point where it now belongs in a newsgroup other than the one where the first message was posted.

Revising Subject Header Lines

An important thing to do, yet often overlooked.

■ Know when it's appropriate to change the subject.

In many cases, a topic will have taken a tangent away from its original one, and a discussion on some unrelated topic (say, "Is the color of the dinosaur droppings in that big Spielberg film true to life, or just a piece of s**t") will be carried out under a different heading (like, say, "Romance novels set on Venus and the women who read them"). If the topic changes, change the subject line to something a little closer to the topic now under discussion.

On the other hand, don't change the topic too often. If you do, and your messages no longer seem to fit the bboard you're sending it to, many readers of that bboard will avoid what they think is an unrelated topic. This is a shame if your post really *is* relevant.

Sometimes, when you do change the subject header, you may wish to list what the previous topic was as well. For example, if the topic being discussed under "Cider vs. Lemonade" had strayed to an in-depth examination of the habits of rabbits, you might want to change the subject to "Rabbit Habits (was: Cider vs. Lemonade)," which would allow those who are following the discussion under one heading to continue to follow it under the new heading.

How to Learn More About Bboard Manners

Once you decide what newsgroup(s) are relevant to your question, make sure you're not asking questions that are frequently asked and answered.

■ Get the FAQs (Frequently Asked Questions).

In addition to looking at recent traffic in the group, check whether your question is included in a FAQ list. By always reading the FAQ before delving into any new newsgroup, you increase your chances of maintaining good cybermanners in that newsgroup. FAQs are posted to each bboard periodically. If you can't find a FAQ on the bboard, re-read Mr. Kent's great Internet book—particularly the parts about FTP and Gopher. Most FAQs are generally accessible via FTP or Gopher, and are archived at rtfm.mit.edu, in directory /pub/USENET/your.group.name.

Q & A on Bboard Manners

So you've read the chapter, and you still have some questions? Try some of these questions and answers. They may clarify some gray areas. (Note that some of these items are derived from the actual FAQ list for USENET's "soc.singles" newsgroup.)

Q: Is it proper manners to post every day to a newsgroup, or should I give others a chance?

You can post as often as you want, as long as you are contributing in some way. Others will still be able to post, regardless of how often you do.

If you start to abuse the posting privilege, however, that's a different story. Sending a thousand messages in one day, for example, may get you hate mail and even threats of removal from your online service. But since it is doubtful you could justify so many messages, the "contribute" rule should keep you in check.

Q: Can I post to as many groups as I want?

Yes. But again, don't abuse; if you do go overboard, others will let you know.

Q: What if I don't like any of the current discussions or just find them all boring?

On the net, as in real life, you're better off working constructively to change something you don't like, rather than just complaining about it. If you'd like to talk about something else, post a message about it, and add enough thoughts about it that the other contributors will have something to nibble on.

In general, the worst thing you can do is post a message along the lines of "This group sucks." Remember: the people posting to and reading newsgroups are real people, and tend to react rather like people would if you were to walk into a party and sulk in the corner, loudly shouting out "This party sucks!" every few minutes while everyone around you is busily enjoying themselves.

If the messages aren't to your liking, either try to contribute positively toward making the group more the way you'd like it to be, or locate another group that is more to your liking. Just announcing your displeasure is unlikely to motivate the other participants to post things you'll want to read; they must be enjoying the current tone and content of their newsgroup, or they wouldn't be contributing to it.

Q: I finally worked up the courage to post my first message, and nobody responded to it. Do you think that other bboard users are conspiring to ignore me?

Most netters are far too disorganized to conspire against anyone. Most messages don't generate responses anyway, otherwise the volume of a typical newsgroup would be even greater than it is. You may need to post a few messages before anyone responds to something you've written.

If you want to maximize your chances of getting a response, try to make sure your articles contain room for others to respond; that is, they should invite others to add their thoughts to yours, and (ideally) say something new and different that will get the attention of your readers. Sometimes messages can be overly thorough, covering the whole subject so authoritatively there's nothing left for anyone to say; no response to a message doesn't mean people aren't reading it or aren't interested by it.

Q: I just posted an article and got flamed—when will I be able to show my face in public again?

You can show it right away (but you might consider not revealing it by posting a .GIF file of your face to that group). Realize that most people flame articles, not people. You could post two messages in one day and have one flamed mercilessly, and the other lauded with emoticon roses by the same people. Just because someone flamed you for something you said doesn't mean the person in question hates you—the best thing to do is just take it all in stride and keep going.

Q: What if my site (i.e., my online service) doesn't carry a particular newsgroup?

Even if your site doesn't carry a given group, it's still possible to post to it. Of course, it may be frustrating not being able to read the messages appearing on the group, but you can at least get responses back in e-mail form. Several "mail-to-news gateways" exist that will take e-mail messages you send them and post them to any group you indicate.

Q: What kinds of articles should I post?

One cannot give a definitive answer that covers all bboards. However, if you think of most bboards as the electronic version of a cocktail party crossed with a radio talk show, you'll get your writing muse in the right (and right-brain) frame of mind. Appropriate posts should be both interactive and entertaining—that is, their content should both invite the participation of others in the electronic conversation and be entertaining to its readers. You might reply to another contributor's post and add an observation that sheds light on a different aspect of the issue under discussion (or just makes some people out there laugh and shoot milk out of their nose).

In general, the best way to get a positive response on any group is to post something that will pique the interest of the other readers and entertain them as well.

Q: Sometimes a bboard can feel intimidating—like everybody knows everyone else and it's hard to just jump in to all the ongoing conversations.

Remember that every poster had to post his or her first message sometime—and that it's no more difficult for you to press the follow-up key than it is for anyone else. Sometimes it helps just to lurk (read the newsgroup for a while)—get a feel for what's going on, what the other posters are like, what topics have already been beaten to death, and what insights, knowledge, and experience you might be able to add that others might not think of. When you do decide to leap in and post something, don't be discouraged if you don't get a response right away, or even if you get a negative response—after all, the net is an imperfect medium and it's easy to be misunderstood, so don't feel bad if you sometimes don't get your ideas across in quite the way you had intended. If you keep your cool and continue participating, people will get to know you, you'll get to know them, and misunderstandings will become less frequent.

Q: Someone just did something wrong on a bboard (violating the rules for that newsgroup). Should I scorch the dweeb's shorts with a flame?

It depends. If you can think of a wonderfully witty, entertaining, and non-offensive way to flame the person who behaved "wrong," it's probably OK to do so. Otherwise it's not generally worth the trouble of putting up a public post about it for the whole world to read. It might be better just to send a note to the poster in e-mail suggesting his/her behavior was uncool.

Summary Points

As I did in the e-mail rules chapter, I will summarize bboard manners with its most important rules (those with the widest relevance):

- Avoid posting messages of a personal or emotional nature or those devoid of real content.
- Don't post others' e-mail without permission.
- Avoid the urge to flame minor errors.
- Target the right audience, and avoid crossposting.
- Be specific, yet not overly wordy, in subject lines.
- Summarize what you are following up.
- Honor requests for "e-mail only" replies, and for anonymity.

chapter 5

More Manners Matters: Do's and Don'ts for Other Cybertasks

In This Chapter

Here I discuss other aspects of net behavior that must follow certain cybermanners rules. You'll read about:

- Electronic message management.
- Disk storage (file) management.
- Telnet (visiting other sites on the net).
- Ftp (file transfers to and from other sites on the net).
- Mailing-list discussion groups.

I will explain the basics of these net features (more details can be culled from other Internet basics books), then discuss some of the rules for proper manners in these areas.

Should It Stay or Should It Go: Managing Mailbox Messages

The content and maintenance of your electronic mailbox is your responsibility. Your mailbox can get overcrowded and unmanageable. Eventually it might remind you of a junk closet so stuffed that every time you open the door, something crashes down on your head. To minimize e-mail headaches, clean out your mailbox as often as necessary. Here's some helpful hints:

- Check e-mail daily, and remain within your limited *disk quota*. Online services usually provide commands for finding out about the specifics (including disk quota) of your account.

- Delete unwanted messages as soon as possible; they take up disk storage.

- Keep messages remaining in your electronic mailbox to a minimum.

- Mail messages can be downloaded or extracted to files, then to disks for future reference.

- Never assume that no one can read your e-mail except yourself; others may be able to read or access your mail (it's sort of like having an Internet KGB). Never send or keep anything you would not mind seeing on the evening news.

- If you'd like a hard copy (a printed version) of a message—or if you just hate trees—you can print your e-mail message before deleting it from the system.

A Place for My Stuff: Managing Disk Storage

Many net services let users store files in disk space allocated to their account. Since you can gather files from many sources (from saved bboard posts, e-mail, and files uploaded from your home computer), many can accumulate over time.

Since most users have rather limited space, files must be monitored carefully; the content and maintenance of a user's *disk storage* area is again the user's responsibility. Follow these rules:

- Keep files to a minimum. Delete as soon as possible.

- Download any files you want to keep to your personal computer's hard drive, or to diskettes, then delete.

- Print if you need a hard copy—then delete.

- Routinely and frequently scan your system for viruses—especially when receiving or downloading files from other systems. Preventing the spread of a virus is good cyberhygiene, and cleanliness is another form of good manners.

Net Navigation: Rules for Telnet

Telnet is a program provided by some net vendors that allows a user of one system to "*Tel*eport" (wow, how Trekkish!) over the Inter*net* to another system on the net. One useful analogy is to view Telnetting as a "virtual Sunday drive" from a starting point (your online service) to a final destination (the computer or service you are Telnetting to). Once at your final destination, you can usually do just about anything you could do "at home" (with some restrictions for security reasons).

Just as most seasoned travelers know how to watch for and avoid basic gaffes in new culture areas, you can avoid Telnet-related problems by following some handy heuristics, such as:

- Download and review instructions locally; it's gauche to tie up ports trying to figure out the system. Many Telnettable services have documentation files available online (or via file transfer, as you'll see in the next section).

- Be courteous to other users seeking information; in Telnet terms, efficiency with time is a true courtesy. Remain on the system only long enough to get your information, then exit from the system. If you don't exhibit good Telnet manners, your net provider could possibly revoke Telnet access.

▌ Screen-captured data or information should be downloaded to your personal computer's hard disk or to diskettes.

Shifting Bits: Rules for File Transfers

Anonymous FTP, or simply FTP, deals with file transfers (FTP = "file transfer protocol"). FTP is a way to access files stored on the Internet and retrieve them over the net—that is, download them to your computer or your online service's disk. For a quick illustration, here's a sample Internet command sequence to retrieve a FAQ about a game called Quayle, with handy translations on the right:

> FTP xyz.school.edu	(connect to a site; a message follows)
> anonymous	(type this when it asks for your name)
> <your e-mail address>	(type your address as the password)
> cd /pub/usenet	(go to the directory you want to be in)
> cd rec.games.Quayle	(go one level down)
> dir	(look at a DIRectory of what's there)
> get r.g.Quayle_FAQ	(get the FAQ file)
> quit	(stop this crazy thing!)

Now some rules for proper FTPing:

▌ Respond to the PASSWORD prompt with your e-mail address. This is done so that, if that site chooses, it can track the level of FTP usage. If your e-mail address causes an error, enter **GUEST** for the next PASSWORD prompt.

- If you don't have FTP access, you can often send e-mail to an FTP-by-mail server. Try putting the single word **help** in the body of the message. A help file will then be e-mailed to you, explaining ways you might be able to get the files you want by other (non-FTP) methods. A common alternative: many servers exist on the net that can e-mail you almost any file you want.

- Always virus-check files you get via FTP. Who knows where it's been! In general, whenever you put a new "foreign" file on your system (whether it's your net disk or your home computer's disk), virus-checking is a smart idea.

- When possible, limit your downloads, especially if they're large (one or more megabytes), to after normal business hours—both locally and for the remote FTP host. The preferred time is late in the evening.

- Adhere to time restrictions as requested by archive sites. Think in terms of the current time at the site that's being visited, not in terms of your local time.

- It's the user's responsibility, when downloading programs, to check for copyright or licensing agreements. If the program is beneficial to your use, pay any author's registration fee. If you have any doubt, don't copy it; there have been many instances of copyrighted software finding its way into FTP archives. If you need tech support for any downloaded programs, request it from the originator of the application. Remove unwanted programs from your systems.

- Use local servers when possible. Some FTP sites have *dedicated mailservers* that will send you files only from that site. It causes less network load to use local FTP servers where they exist.

- Seek special programs and servers when you need help. If you don't know exactly what you're looking for, or exactly where it is, there are programs and servers that can help you. It's poor cybermanners to just FTP lots of files in the hope that some may be what you want—besides the storage cost, your time using FTP bogs down the net.

Mailing-list Discussion Groups

Basically, *mailing lists* are a cross between e-mail and bboards. How it generally works: first you add your name to a mailing list that contains many names of like-minded people (that is, netters united by their interest in a certain topic—sounds like USENET and other bboards, right?). After this process of *subscribing* to such a list, a server machine periodically sends documents dealing with the topic of that list to all subscribers—and does so via e-mail.

Mailing-list discussion groups use a similar distribution method. You can send e-mail to a central location (the server), and from there everyone on the list gets a copy of the e-mail (sent by the trusty server).

Some rules for mailing-list manners:

- Subscription to Interest Groups or Discussion Lists should be kept to a minimum, and should not exceed what your disk quota (or you) can handle. Some mailing lists have low rates of traffic, others can flood your mailbox with several hundred mail messages per day. Before you revel in such apparent popularity, consider: Numerous messages by multiple users, coming in from various listservers or mailing lists, require extensive system processing, which can tie up valuable resources—which can be very inconsiderate.

- If you can get all the info you need on a topic from a bboard, use that method instead of mailing lists. All other things being equal, it's more efficient simply to post information and have people read it than to have a machine send the same information to a multitude of readers. But if the mailings add to your satisfaction, by all means use them. Just (to paraphrase an ex-President) be prudent.

- Keep your questions and comments relevant to the focus of the discussion group.

- Resist the temptation to "flame" others on the list. Remember that these discussions are "public," and meant for *constructive* exchanges. Treat the others on the list as you would want them to treat you.

- When replying to a message posted to a discussion group, check the address to be certain it's going to the intended location (person or group). With some groups, you simply reply, and it goes to the mailing-list server automatically. With some other groups, however, you have to enter the correct address (if you simply reply, the message doesn't get added to the group).

- When signing up for a group, save your subscription confirmation letter for reference.

- When going away for more than a week, unsubscribe or suspend mail from your mailing lists.

- If you can respond to someone else's question, do so through e-mail. Twenty people answering the same question on a large list can fill your mailbox (and those of everyone else on the list) quickly.

- Use your own personal e-mail account; *don't* use a shared office account to subscribe.

- Any requests regarding administrative tasks (such as being added to or removed from a list) should be made to the appropriate area, not the list itself. Other people on the list are not interested in your desire to be added or deleted; getting errant mail can, of course, be annoying.

- Occasionally subscribers who are not familiar with proper manners will submit requests to SUBSCRIBE or UNSUBSCRIBE directly to the list itself. Be tolerant of this activity. It is incorrect, but not the end of the world. In addition, you can also provide some useful advice to the newbie as opposed to being critical. However, if the same person does this over and over, then you can consider taking other action. Dust off your fireproof coveralls and see the chapter on flames, coming up next on this same station :-).

Summary Points

Here are some highlights from this chapter—some of the most important rules for electronic message management, disk storage (file) management, Telnetting to other sites on the net, file transfers, and mailing list discussion groups:

- Delete unwanted e-mail immediately; it takes up disk storage. In general, keep files to a minimum; download them to your personal computer whenever possible, then delete them from your online service account.

- Never assume that your files can be read by no one except yourself.

- Be courteous to other users seeking information; don't stay on too long.

- Subscription to Interest Groups or Discussion Lists should be kept to a minimum, and should not exceed what your disk quota (or you) can handle.

- Keep your questions and comments relevant to the focus of a mailing list, and resist the temptation to "flame" others on the list.

- When replying to a message posted to a discussion group, check the address to be certain it's going to the intended location (person or group).

- Requests regarding administrative tasks (e.g., add/remove from a list) should be made to the appropriate area, not the list itself.

part

Popular Problems and Questionable Net Behavior

Now we've covered what you can do with e-mail and bulletin boards, and generally how to do these activities in a *proper* manner. In this part of the book I look at the flip side, discussing well-known general *abuses* of communications that often occur along the evolving information superhighway. Covered are the most common mistakes—some unintentional, some not—that netters make using net-based communication.

What are the worst violations one can commit? Like a lot of cybermanners, that's relative—it depends on your point of view.

We will try to focus on the most common cybermanners violations in this part of the book. These include: flaming, spamming, jamming, and whamming (the four biggies), plus other important cyberproblems. The final chapter covers a potpourri of interesting personality types on the net—see if there's someone in there you recognize.

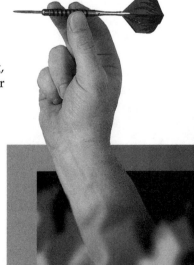

chapter 6

Flaming: When Messages Get Too Emotional or Negative

In This Chapter
- Some flame basics, and the causes of flames
- Some advice for dealing with flames, and protecting yourself from them
- What to do when you get the urge to flame
- Flame-in-a-box: a fill-in-the-blanks flame form, plus my own (sarcastic?) version
- Some Q & A on flames

Here we delve into the behavior most associated with questionable cybermanners: flaming. And, of course, the agent of the behavior, and arguably the most well-known class of net messages: the flame itself. This may be a hot topic, but you won't get burned. (Sorry. Bad flame puns are an additional fire hazard.)

Some Flame Basics

Don't worry, you cannot get real fire into or out of your computer (unless you reside in L.A. and the coming Great Quake drops a roof on your Mac—then all bets are off). However, a phenomenon called *flaming* has appeared on the net.

Flame messages are, in general, those with a higher-than-average level of emotion (usually angry) or negative spirit. They're usually overladen with opinion in lieu of helpful content, often go on far too long (again, more than the average message you find on the net), or are too harsh or express views in an unacceptable manner. Sometimes the message's flame-like quality is deliberate and calculated, sometimes it unconsciously sneaks into a message, and sometimes it is a one-time outburst that the sender regrets for the rest of his or her life.

However you choose to define or categorize flames, their frequency has prompted some to dub the net the "Electronic Wild West." Have you ever received e-mail from a total stranger that blew you away with its rudeness, its downright cheek? Did you then rip off a saucy reply at the speed of light to relieve the stress? Did the exchange begin to resemble artillery salvos on all fronts? If this all sounds too familiar, take heart, for it happens all the time in the Electronic Wild West. You are smack in the middle of a flame war—typically formed when a flame sparks another flame, then another, followed by a cascade of them.

What Causes Flames?

Some of the reasons put forth to explain the origin of flame-like behavior include the list I'm about to present. All these factors, when taken together, create a situation that you must constantly be on the lookout for when you use electronic mail systems. Bear in mind, however, that the relative importance of these various factors has yet to be proven beyond a shadow of a doubt. I doubt they ever will be. Still, they should help you understand the flame phenomenon.

- The anonymity of the e-mail medium.

  When using high tech, it's easy to forget you're dealing with a fellow citizen. While e-mail is a great equalizer—bypassing first impressions and prejudices based on personal appearance—it is also words floating in a digital void which have little perceptible connection to a person with blood pressure.

  Persons who send electronic mail over a network to folks they may not know may feel freer to communicate feelings more forcefully and colorfully than they would to friends or associates. For instance, if no one knows "Al at ACME-Net," Al may feel "safe" to say anything, with little risk of wrathful consequences.

- This medium lacks immediate feedback from body language, interruptions, or other cues we have developed as a society to aid the intercommunication process.

  This lack of "paralingual" cues contributes to frequent misinterpretation of messages. For example, all you may see are words on the computer screen that make you boil. You cannot read the sender's body language or hear the inflection in their words (which might indicate an attempt at irony or humor instead of sarcasm or anger).

- It is difficult to tell a message's level of formality from its appearance; to a considerable degree, they all look the same.

  Again, this relates to the number and types of language cues, which are more subtle than telling the difference between a scrawled note and a formal memorandum.

- Attempts at humor, irony, sarcasm, and wit are often misinterpreted.

  This is so partly because of the lack of cues to the level of formality, because of the nature of writing, and because most participants are not professional writers.

- Unlike other modes of written communication, online interaction rarely allows some intervening time to blunt the edge of a response, or to allow reconsideration.

A written letter may lie on someone's desk for several days or weeks before they respond to it. In contrast, the ease of creating an immediate "reply" to an electronic message (often easiest to do immediately upon viewing the message) biases the e-mail user to respond immediately, "off the top of his/her head." Often the kinder answers don't live up there.

- Telephone calls and personal conversations that involve hasty or ill-chosen words fade with time. Electronic messages containing similar infelicities have a *permanence* to them. They sit around in electronic inboxes, or are printed out and remain tangible, and can even be printed in a manner (inkjet, laser, or typesetting) that gives them an aura of formality and importance that was never intended.

If you find that you're getting flamed a lot, you may need to consider your presentation. Even if you're saying perfectly reasonable things, a lot of people will have trouble with what you're saying if you

- Sound like you think and speak for all humanity.

or

- Keep saying the same thing over and over without listening.

Many netters forget to pay real attention to how people are responding to them, and so fail to respond thoughtfully in turn.

Advice for Dealing with Flames

How should one respond to a flame? Is there one best way? A more intelligent response involves *filtering*, where an e-mail message or bboard posting from a particular address is deleted automatically. If someone always flames you, just "kill" them (delete their messages). If you don't have access to automatic filtering, do it manually; scan for the info your ideal "automatic filter" program would look for, and delete that stuff yourself.

So you still want to know how to stay on the safe side and avoid the scorch marks of flaming? Most of the previous rules I presented for proper cybermanners apply; if you do well in those areas the chances are greatly reduced that you'll exhibit flame-generating behavior. Still, there is a chance, so here are some ideas for avoiding the heat:

- Approach an e-mail contact with someone new with eyes wide open.

- Answer messages promptly, if only to simply acknowledge their receipt, so the sender is not left wondering if their message got through the maze of wires and protocols.

- Clearly identify yourself and your affiliations.

- Keep messages brief. Most people would rather read long passages on paper. One screen is better than two is better than three; any more is a dissertation.

- Be sure to label strongly worded statements as opinion.

- Risk a little friendliness. It doesn't hurt to throw in the odd "please," either.

- Be careful with attempts at humor, sarcasm, satire, and other witticisms. Unless you know your correspondent well and they are plugged into your e-mail mannerisms, what strikes your funny bone might seem like impudence, witlessness, or worse, to someone else.

- Sleep on messages that get your goat. This admonishment applies to e-mail *or* bboard posts. Don't respond until sober second thoughts set in. Ask for clarification before diving into the abyss of hurt feelings. What you see as a gratuitous insult could be a mere misunderstanding or a sloppy choice of words. Give your e-mail correspondent the benefit of the doubt. Assume they have professional integrity, and reply to the business of the message the next day with a clear head. If you get another nasty note, even Saint Francis would not begrudge you the termination of further correspondence. There's nothing an e-mail bully likes less than to be ignored by a morally superior personage ;-).

- If an e-mail interaction becomes strained and stilted, resort to more natural mammalian forms of communication. A meeting with eye contact and some preening and posturing can do wonders for an e-mail correspondence that is fraying at the edges.

- Remember that with e-mail, unlike the telephone, you *can* organize your thoughts properly and get it right the first time.

- Master *message-recalling commands* if your e-mail system provides them. These allow you to retrieve posted e-mail that is still unread. Even with the best intentions and a doctorate in e-mail etiquette, it's easy to commit indiscretions because spontaneity is in the nature of the medium.

- Don't be shy about breaking up a (flame) fight. Here is an actual example from an actual USENET post (edited down, with personal info altered or omitted):

    Newsgroups: news.newusers.questions
    Subject: Re: Some More Thoughts About Newcomers

    Person One (person1@blah.blah.blah.edu) wrote:

    > :   Recently I posted an article on here which ... said
    > :   that beginners should neither be seen nor heard.

    Person Two (person2@twiddle.dee.net) wrote:

    > ...   Your posting isn't worth further waste of time
    > ...   and energy for additional comment.

    Please, let me re-post:

    ... use the appropriate newsgroup. May I humbly remind you that "news.newusers.questions" is for questions OF NEW USERS about how to use the net.

    For discussions ... ABOUT new users and their access to the net, ... use the "news.admin.policy" and "news.future" newsgroups.

    And, please, make friendship and love rather than flame wars :-(

> Dr. <Name Deleted>
>
> Please correct me if I'm wrong!
>
> Make love, not flame wars. :-)

Doctor Deleted was not only explaining the rules of this newsgroup, but was also attempting to douse a developing flame war before it got out of hand. Feel free to emulate this gallant behavior.

Flame Retardants: Protecting Yourself Against the Heat

There is no universal foolproof method of protecting yourself from flames. However, some netters do include disclaimers to discourage others from flaming them. These are used if the sender thinks there is the possibility of "flammable content" in their message.

Here is an example I found intriguing (edited from an article posted on the net). It appeared, as most disclaimers do, at the end of a user's message:

> Disclaimer: Everything in this article is my opinion only.
> [This user's] College ... has nothing to do with any of it.
> ... If this review makes you mad enough to flame, flame yourself. If you flame me and as a result I do something rash, my wife and kids will sue you.

This disclaimer almost sounds like a flame itself! But perhaps it is an attempt to "fight fire with fire," in a virtual sense. The user, who wasn't an expert on the topic discussed in the message (and knew it), tried to head off any possible flame responses with this short addendum.

Note that, since no emoticons were used, it is impossible to tell for sure if the "sue you" warning is real, or just a kind of virtual "Beware of Dog" sign without a dog behind it. In fact, much of this disclaimer seems to walk the edge between real warning and so much overkill it must be part tongue in cheek. (The last line, to me, reads like a joke attempt—but it is not obvious enough to make the reader sure of this. What do you think?)

One could argue that its ambiguous nature is what makes this disclaimer a good flame retardant for its author. (But is arguing what we really want to do? :-)

When You Get the Urge to Flame...

Flaming is not always 100% "bad" cybermanners. If handled properly, it can be OK to flame. The main thing to avoid is *personal* attacks on people. There are a number of techniques to actually make a flame "palatable," such as...

- If you must flame—that is, you are a "cyber-pyro" (hey, maybe a good name for a rock band?)—label your hot message carefully and clearly.

    This shows you are aware of your writing, and care enough about your reader(s) to give them warnings about content. For example: you can use what I call the "caustic clapper." That is, begin your remarks with FLAME ON; end them with FLAME OFF.

    It also helps to put flame-warning labels in subject headers, too. Example:

    FLAME ON:

    I strongly believe that the insensitive person from Antarctica should stop posting such long-winded (and boring) messages.

    FLAME OFF.

- Humor us—be humorous! People forgive a lot when they're entertained. Just ask Ronald Reagan (just kidding, Gipper :-). Also, humorous flames are more likely to be read all the way through.

Flaming: When Messages Get Too Emotional or Negative

- Let's get personal—NOT! Don't attack a person (that is, their virtual online persona); stick to ideas. Ninety-nine times out of 100, it's ideas you're concerned with anyway. This is one of the surest ways to avoid a flame war, because ideas tend to be less "flammable" than personal pride.

- Don't take it personally. The flip side of the previous rule. Now it's *your* turn to stave off a flame war. Can you meet the challenge? Even if someone appears to be attacking you personally, it's probably just your ideas or facts. Remember: sticks and stones... (hey, maybe Fulghum is right, we DO learn everything we need to know in kindergarten).

- You don't have to aim a flame at anyone at all. You can just eloquently and passionately state your opinions as a kind of soliloquy. Of course, this applies to bboards and everything *except* personal e-mail—since you have to send the latter *to* someone, silly! :-)

- Be aware of where you flame. Some bboards are more tolerant (and more flammable) than others. Know which is which. Also, some services (such as the WELL) actually have bboards designed for flames (like the Flame Box); if so, send flames there, or try to set up your own version of a Flame Box on your service if there isn't one already.

- Consider what net section you are flaming on. The thinner the bandwidth, the bigger the violation of cybermanners if you flame. For example, an Internet chat channel (discussed in Chapter 9) is a terrible place for a long flame because interactions are done line by line, interactively, among many people.

- Resist the temptation to fire off a response. You can *write* the response, but file it away, and wait 24 hours. Reconsider the response later, in the light of a new day (and perhaps a rereading and reinterpretation of the original message).

▉ Use alternative media to break the cycle of message-and-response. A telephone call or personal conversation can do wonders, when voice inflection, body language, eye contact, and all the other cues we've developed can take effect. This is especially important if electronic communications seem to be becoming too formal and stilted.

Flame in a Box: the Semi-official Standard Flame Form

We all like others to take the drudgery out of our lives, right? And since you're reading this book, I assume you're into automating repetitive tasks, yes? And sometimes we're just too l-a-z-y to whip up that snappy rejoinder flame or soliloquy.

Luckily there's good news! For you, my kind reader, here is a form—adopted on several areas of the net—which should prove useful, as well as entertaining:

To :_____

I have read your recent post concering
_____.

I regret that due to severe time constraints I am unable to respond to your posting directly. However, I would like to advise you that I believe that your posting:

____ contains an unacceptable number of errors in:
    ____ logic
    ____ fact
    ____ spelling/grammar
____ is based on stereotypes of:
    ____ race, ethnic, national origin
    ____ gender differences
    ____ sexual orientation / preferences
    ____ regionalisms

Flaming: When Messages Get Too Emotional or Negative

___ employer and/or school affiliations
___ religious affiliation/non-affiliation
___ violates commonly accepted net standards concerning:
    ___ signature size
    ___ posting to subjects not of general interest
    ___ editing of quoted material
    ___ posting of copyrighted material
___ is uninteresting because it
    ___ contains hackneyed expressions
    ___ contains outright stupidities
    ___ is inherently self-contradictory
    ___ reflects inadequate intellectual development or maturity
    ___ reiterates points made better by others
    ___ is a gratuitous attack on an obvious provocateur
    ___ reflects serious misunderstandings concerning:
        ___ the basic functioning of this list
        ___ the basic purposes of the Internet
        ___ the basic nature of _____
        ___ basic human nature
        ___ the basic nature of computers
        ___ the profit motive of vendors
        ___ others' interest in your thoughts
        ___ copyright
___ is an unjustified, unprovoked, and thoughtless response to my previous posting, which was careful, moderate, and well-reasoned.

Author disclaimer: I did not create this form from scratch; it was posted on the net and provided for you as a public service. So don't flame me if you don't like it! (Even if you wanna use the form to do it :.)

Flame in a Box II: My Own Version

I happen to have my own prefab flame form, which you can also use. I hear there are versions like this floating around the net, but this is my original recipe for retribution.

> Whenever there are multiple words, just select one. I know you'll find it effective. Sprinkle with expletives, and add a pinch of sarcasm where needed. (Actually, I hope you'll realize that the whole thing is *already* sarcastic!) Serve immediately—preferably piping hot.
>
> Dear (Newbie/Lurker/Idiot/Freak/Loser/Spec-o'-Dust):
>
> You are wrong. I am right. If you respond to this, all your arguments will be wrong as well, so don't even bother. In fact, getting off the net and getting a life might be good advice for you.
>
> Sincerely and perfectly,
>
> (Your Name Here, or
> "The Most Divinely Perfect Netter of All Time")

Summary Points

- Flaming is a common practice on the net. Some think of flames as bullets in the new "Electronic Wild West." Think of this chapter as a sheriff who's also the town barkeep—full of advice on doing things right, pardner.

- Not all flames are necessarily bad. The key to not getting burned (and avoiding burning others) is figgerin' out how you deal with and construct flames. I reckon this chapter's given plenty of advice on these here matters.

- Flaming's got plenty of outlaw cousins that have just started ridin' into town; the next chapters will deal with these, nice and slow-like. Go south, young man (or woman—let's be PC, now, ya hear?)—to the next page.

chapter 7

Spamming, Jamming, and Whamming, Oh My! More Cyberproblems

In This Chapter

Although flaming is arguably the most common cyberproblem, there are other dubious behaviors often exhibited by net users, which usually lead to problems and violate cybermanners to some degree. Activities discussed in this chapter include

- Spamming—mass postings to many bboards in parallel.

- Jamming—not radio interference, not impromptu guitar sessions, but the clogging of the net with noise of various kinds.

- Whamming—often severe "cybermanners-impoverished" actions, usually from many users in parallel, made in response to netter actions.

- A group of others—let it be among the surprises that spur you to read on!

Spamming: Mass Postings

Spamming refers to mass postings. This behavior is usually undertaken by commercial organizations trying to sell to a large audience, which is (as many have discovered) readily available on the net. Another phrase for this could be "net marketing overkill."

A Spamming Story: Canter and Siegel Versus the Net

This case is probably one of the most famous Internet anecdotes to date. It involves two lawyers who tried to capitalize on the net, but found that one can indeed experience backfires on the information superhighway.

The Wall Street Journal, TIME, and other national publications have discussed how Canter and Siegel, a husband-and-wife law firm, found itself scorched by flame mail for blanketing the Internet with advertising for their legal services; their ads were sent to thousands of newsgroups. "People like Canter and Siegel are taking grotesque advantage of liberating technology that supports the free and open exchange of ideas," said the president of one Internet-related business. Howard Rheingold, noted author on "virtual village" issues, compared the effect of the spamming by C & S to "getting 60,000 pieces of junk mail."

The problem of C & S (and many other spamming incidents) goes well beyond just crossposting; others had done this before, without a stormy reaction from the net. Here are some other contributing factors that led to the reaction C & S received (and illustrate why spamming can be so annoying):

- They were advertising a dubious service—"Get a green card for money." (Green cards are free, and there are agencies that can help you get one free.) There is no analog to TV's FCC to help control the netwaves' content.

- When people pointed out to C & S that their actions were inappropriate, the law firm expressed sentiments along the lines of "Tough." To be inconsiderate and then be proud of it tends to tick people off.

- Many saw the C & S ad in the comp.graphics forum, which is designed for technical discussions of computer-graphics issues. Some of this USENET newsgroup's users felt it was already jammed with too many inappropriate posts. C & S compounded the problem; their posts were not only off the topic, but also prompted dozens of follow-up posts.

A helpful analogy concerning C & S (and others like them) is this: Compare the net to a public park. Suppose many community volunteers and monetary contributors work together for years to build swings, play areas, walkways, gardens, chessboard tables, and other facilities for the public to enjoy and use. Along comes a company that puts up a lighted billboard in the middle of the garden, with flashing lights to advertise their product. They say, "It's a public park. We have a right to be here too." But do the advertisers have a right to take advantage of what others spent time, money, and energy to build, especially if those others see the intrusion as tearing down and cheapening their efforts?

Analyzing his defense in more detail, Siegel stated that "[o]ur fate has been that we're making a lot of money. If a bunch of hysterics want to scream and yell and make fools of themselves, then I don't feel they warrant respect." C & S has even decided to launch a new service, Cybersell, to help other businesses do mass "cyber-mailings." The goal of Cybersell is to charge $500 for access to 6,000 newsgroups.

Will Cybersell sell? This depends in part on the reaction of netters; since many vehemently flamed Canter and Siegel, other advertisers might be reluctant to endure the same treatment. Businesses will have to weigh the benefits of mass recognition (and potentially millions of new readers for their ads) against the possibility of backlash from angry netters.

Dealing With Spamming

Those who hated what C & S did flooded the pair's e-mailbox with so much e-mail (both flame and non-flame varieties) that C & S were (in effect) shut out of the net—their online service provider could not handle the e-mail volume. In addition, C & S violated the rules of their provider (which most netters must agree to when signing onto a service), and that provider was compelled to boot them off for that reason as well.

But was the flood of flame mail an example of good cybermanners? That depends. Certainly sending one message to C & S and voicing an opinion is not bad or incorrect—but sending *hundreds* of noise-filled or flaming messages simply fights fire with fire, and doesn't seem much better than the original spamming (IMHO).

Well, the jury is still out on this case. For now, remember this: Once upon a time, mass fax mailings prompted the government to legislate restrictions. Will Internet posting restrictions now occur as well?

Jamming: Overcrowding E-mailboxes and Bboards

There is also a problem with USENET and other net-based bboards becoming overcrowded with *noise*, a phenomenon I refer to as *jamming*. I also use this term to describe overcrowding of personal e-mailboxes or public bboards. The glut can stem from an overabundance of interested users (when there's a sudden news event related to a particular bboard topic), or a too-general topic name (like alt.everything, or misc.words-containing-the-letter-E; I made up these names, but I hope the point is clear).

One behavior that contributes to jamming is *crossposting* (which we met in Chapter 4), where one sends a message to more bboards than a subject warrants, or to unrelated bboards. The problem is that new message threads can evolve, leading to jamming on the unrelated bboards. Of course, the spamming behavior of C & S in the previous section is an extreme example of jamming by crossposting. In general, "noise" leads to a low "meat-to-gristle" ratio in the ongoing online discussion, and simply wastes everyone's valuable time.

Other ways that people purposely or unwittingly contribute to jamming include the dying-kid posts and electronic chain letters mentioned in an earlier chapter. Yet another contributing factor is the number of people who get access to famous people's e-mail addresses, and flood the poor rich folks with e-mail (which is, no offense, junk e-mail to the celeb on the receiving end). A new book by Seth Godin called *E-Mail of the Rich and Famous*, with its listing of many celebrity e-mail addresses, hasn't helped in this regard.

I also use the term jamming to cover *misinformation* spread on the net—jamming the netwaves, if you will.

Examples, Anecdotes, and Commentary

Although the discussion thus far has focused on bboards, e-mail is also vulnerable to jamming problems. When discussing Godin's book in a *Wall Street Journal* article, Dave Barry e-mailed the observation that by using electronic mail "you THINK you're going to be on the Information Superhighway and get information all over the world, but what you actually GET is about 9000 messages that say: 'Are you really (your name)?'" Barry comments further: "In some ways... I like the... U.S. Postal Service Superhighway better. I rarely get letters asking me if I am me."

Writing in *Science Fiction Eye*, another notable author, Bruce Sterling, comments that in the not-too-distant future he may need to change his on-line persona in order to deal with the volumes of unsolicited e-mail he gets. Of course, this would provide him with "a pretty problem in virtual etiquette: Who will get my new address and who will have to be dropped? How will I convince people to maintain the secrecy of my new ID when the whole *raison d'être* of the infobahn is instant access to anybody anywhere anytime?"

Sterling leaves the question hanging, since there is no easy answer yet; perhaps one strategy of future netters will be an automatic "death-and-resurrection" via on-line IDs, where you take a new digital identity once a month, as easily as putting on a new pair of virtual shoes.

"Instant access to anybody, anywhere, anytime" has even reached Washington, D.C. Today you can e-mail President Clinton's net address, but you'll get a form e-mail in reply: "Thank you for writing to President Clinton via electronic mail. The President is committed to integrating this dynamic medium into the White House."

Integrating? Feels more like grating to me—for reasons more practical than political. Imagine if millions of netters used automated replies like this. In some cases there would be legitimate cause to do so, but the vast majority would simply clog e-mailboxes around the world. One e-message causing another to be auto-sent, which could (if cc: lines were not empty) cause a chain reaction of e-mail to be sent. Imagine answering machines talking to each other, and you can see the nightmarish possibilities.

In addition, I know many netters (mostly other writers) who have been disappointed to find that the net is not the wonderful world they thought it would be. Some find the net to be, essentially, a vast wasteland, often full of rude and even vulgar people. And on top of these qualities, there is the perception that very little of substance is being said, that the net is mostly full of idle chatter.

Of course, anecdotes do not a theory make. There are also counter-examples of people using—and loving—net interactions, without having any problems. But there are enough anecdotes to make jamming a problem to be reckoned with.

Advice for Dealing with Jamming

How should jamming be dealt with? Flame the idiot who caused the jam? Not so fast. This "solution" can be just as bad—or worse—than the original problem. Ignoring jamming behavior is one way to get results; remember *extinction* from Psych 101? Sooner or later, those who want replies to the jamming messages they post will probably stop posting if they cannot generate interest.

If ignoring fails, you could try sending polite-yet-firm e-mail to those who seem to be jamming the net. If all this fails, you might tell the jammers you've given their net address to someone just like them. And their real address to that gal who stalks Letterman.

And now for something completely different (or the same, depending on your point of view): some rules to help you *avoid jamming behavior* and keep yourself from becoming an accidental jammer:

- Send e-mail only to relevant people. Some e-mail programs send a reply automatically to every person on the original To: field *and* the original Cc: field. Edit out those names you don't need. Also consider changing the default setting of your e-mail program if it *does* indeed do this.

- Avoid accidentally sending more than one copy of the same message to someone. One way to keep track is to cc: yourself on important messages; then you can always reread the message, and see who you already sent it to by scanning the To: and Cc: fields.

- Use mailing lists carefully. If you send e-mail to one, everyone on the list will get your message. Make sure that's what you want. Remember to send requests to subscribe and unsubscribe to the correct address (which is almost never the same address as the one for the actual list). Also, remember to keep the "welcome to this list" message(s) handy (you usually get one upon subscribing); they contain helpful advice and useful info (like how to unsubscribe when you no longer want to participate in the list).

- Don't introduce noise into the system (i.e., the net). If you take some piece of information and distort it, then send the distorted info out on the net, you've added to the overall jamming state (i.e., noise) of the net. This is how vicious rumors start (gradual mutation of an original fact or idea into a vastly different form, as in the familiar party game of "Telephone"). And if the distortion then causes a flame war, there will be even more noise.

Now some rules to keep in mind for *responding to jammers* who clog the net:

■ Don't blindly accept what you read on the net as truth. Try to verify the information—and its source—as often as you can. If you pass along incorrect information, you are allowing the net noise to continue (whether you intend it or not).

■ Don't flame—inform. Send a polite, yet stern, message to the person you feel is jamming the "netwaves"—but be sure the person is really doing this. Gather some evidence—which you can then summarize in your message to back you up. Inform the other party so they learn something, and hopefully will change their behavior.

If you find yourself swamped with too much e-mail, here's some advice for *dealing with jammed e-mailboxes:*

■ Prioritize your responses, and adjust length accordingly. Although it may hurt at first, you may have to shorten your replies. The less important the message is, or the less familiar you are with the person e-mailing you, the shorter the response will have to be (and the less time you should spend creating it).

■ Use automated reply programs, but sparingly. Such programs are like specialized on-line secretaries—very useful when you are away on vacation and you want people to know where you are. They become less beneficial when crafting an informed reply is important. (Ask your sysadmin for more info on availability and usage of such autoreply software.)

■ Be careful not to use autoreplies all the time (that is, not automatically for all cases), or else you too may become an accidental jammer. For example, if one person e-mailed you but a hundred were on the cc: line, an automated response sent to everyone may not be what you had in mind.

One way to deal with e-mail overload if you're rich and famous (or just want to act that way): Have two on-line IDs—one for public consumption, and the other for your closest and most important friends and associates. Then you can use automated response for the first ID and not the second. Another idea (possibly better, and more workable for most users): set up different addresses for different functions. This is especially useful for businesses; think of voice-mailboxes as an analogy. For example:

info@spammaster.com	general purposes
support@spammaster.com	customer service and support
president@spammaster.com	the big boss's public address
joeschmoe@spammaster.com	the big boss's private address

You get the idea. (But *ask* Joe before posting that last one.)

Whamming: Harsh Reaction Tactics

Whamming is how I refer to the heavy-duty responses some netters use to clobber others (as in "Wham! I got that sucker with tons of flame mail from my friends"). These responses are often hasty and/or nasty. Whamming is usually done when one or more netters feel that someone (or some group of someones) has violated cybermanners; the reaction is often taken up by many netters in parallel.

One whamming tactic: *mail bombs*, the use of mass mailings or the flooding of e-mailboxes (public or personal). This has been done in response to spamming (such as the Canter and Siegel incident), but smacks of spamming itself. In general, it is almost never good cybermanners to fight fire with fire.

Can whamming be viewed as acceptable cybermanners if it is done in response to another violation? In most cases, I would say no—especially when whamming is as bad or worse than the original perceived "offense." Take grievances to the system administrator, or to higher-ups at your net service provider. Until some system of cyberpolice is implemented on the net (and some feel this may never or should never occur), this is the best course of action. That, and trying some of the e-mail and bboard advice given earlier in this book. (Okay, I'll stop plugging myself!)

Summary Points

- Avoid spamming; it jams the net and most people despise it. Any potential gains in visibility for a company can be offset by the flame mail received.

To avoid being a jammer:

- Only send e-mail to relevant people.
- Do not send multiple copies of the same message.
- Use mailing lists carefully.
- Don't introduce noise into the system (i.e., the net).

How to respond to jammers:

- Don't blindly accept what you read on the net as truth. Try to verify the information and its source as often as you can.
- Don't flame—inform.

To handle jamming of your own e-mailbox:

- Prioritize your responses and adjust length accordingly.
- Use automated reply programs, but sparingly.

chapter 8

"Do You Know Me?": Interesting Net Personality Types

In This Chapter

Do you want to know what kinds of interesting behavior occurs online that doesn't easily fall into classes of good or bad cybermanners? Here are the main behavior patterns covered in this chapter:

- Anonymous Versus Famous: real and fake identities on the net
- The Clark-Kent-to-Superman Effect: when the shy turn bold
- The Jekyll-and-CyberHyde Effect: when the nice turn mean
- Bitpickers: netters who nitpick, overdetail, or overanalyze
- Funny Fiends: those who overdo humor, and how to deal with them
- Info Addicts: "Get away from that tube!" revisited

Chapter 8

■ll The Gump Effect: "stupid is as stupid does" on the net

■ll Robocomm: automated agents online

Note that for each section that follows (except the first), I constructed hypothetical comments ("virtual confessions," if you will) to illustrate some of the feelings typically felt by folks who exhibit these behaviors. You'll learn about the behavior, and get advice for dealing with it.

Anonymous Versus Famous: Real and Fake Identities on the Net

For better or worse, anonymity is a fact of life on the net. Being anonymous is possible with any e-mail address. Some netters always act under assumed or fake names—either fully anonymous, or pseudonymous (using a pseudonym). In addition, some netters constantly change their online label; I call this third class "chameleonymous."

Those people who choose not to use their real identity (or something close to it) on the net can be categorized in many ways. One breakdown:

■ll Class 1: nonfamous people who like acting as another gender (i.e., gender benders).

■ll Class 2: people have to avoid using their real names on the net due to their fame. Ironic, isn't it? In real life they are so well known that on the net they must become totally unknown.

■ll Class 3: anyone who is anonymous or pseudonymous to hide poor (or downright nasty) cybermanners.

Although there is no scientific proof, most netters-in-the-know agree that a higher percentage of anonymous posters tend to abuse the trust of other (often naive) netters with clever deceptions.

For example, there is the phenomenon of *impostors*. These are netters who, using fake online personas, post messages on bboards. Impostors usually want to generate responses by stating facts or opinions that are either untrue, unproven, or misleading. The goal is often financial gain. A mid-1994 *Newsweek* story focused on impostors who, interacting with fake identities, were paid to create artificial excitement about certain musical groups (or Bogus Band Buzz, if you will). Once "outed," however, the impostors were roundly flamed. Was it worth the money, impostors?

Other abuses commonly perpetrated by anonymous netters include flaming, "mail bombs," and "cyberstalking"—all discussed earlier in this book.

Some Cybermanners Advice

- Be careful what you say; you don't know who's behind a name! For instance, if you're a guy who loves talkin' macho, you never know if the person you're bonding with is *really* male or female. In fact, there's a well-known saying in cyberspace: "on the Internet, no one knows you're a dog." So for Dog's sake, don't make cute canine comedy quips (unless you wanna get bit).

- If you run an online service, develop well-thought-out policies regarding allowable levels of anonymity and how to deal with abuses.

Apple is one online service provider that has taken a stand. They are going to one extreme: according to their sources, users of their new eWorld service must use real identities. Apple claims that this will result in behavior "more conducive to the business environment that eWorld is designed for."

The Clark-to-Superman Effect: When the Shy Turn Bold

The following are some sample confessions of the Clark-to-Superman Syndrome. (Secret identities and bulletproof costumes optional.)

"I can't help it. I feel shy in real life, but when I send e-mail I don't feel as many restrictions. I loosen up."

"Sometimes I reread the e-mail I sent and I seem downright aggressive; depending how long it's been since I sent it, it can be a bit of a shock."

"On the newsgroups, it's like I feel safe to let another side of me come out. But not too much. I still don't reveal certain sides of me in public, even if that public is virtual."

Even when not anonymous or pseudonymous, e-mail gives an extra buffer layer to social interaction on the net that enables some folks to exhibit this kind of behavior pattern. The feeling of displacement from "real F2F (face-to-face) interactions" gives some on the net a feeling of relative freedom to "come out of their shell" and "let their hair down."

Some who act shy in real life can seem much bolder, even aggressive or arrogant, when communicating online. This behavior can increase if someone purposely uses an anonymous or fake online identity.

Advice

- If you get e-mail from a Clark-turned-Superman, take this effect into account when you read and respond. Over time, you can compare several messages to your real-world interactions and judge if this pattern exists, or if someone really is becoming a different person (some really do become more assertive in both their real and personal lives).

  Also, if someone is getting swamped with e-mail (see the "jamming" section in Chapter 7), their terse responses may *seem* sometimes to indicate overconfidence, or even arrogance, when in fact they are just being brief to save time.

▮▮▮ If you feel you fit this pattern, there is nothing overtly wrong with it, as long as you don't slip into more severe harassing or flaming patterns. Rereading your e-mail a few times before sending is always a good idea, but for those fitting this type it is especially good advice.

The Jekyll and CyberHyde Effect: When the Nice Turn Mean

Beware: going online can act like the good doctor's nasty elixir, sometimes perplexing the netters who are prone to its effects:

> "I don't mean to be mean. It just happens, I guess. I see something I don't like and it's so darn easy to fire off a quick comment. I don't have time to censor or edit back my comments."

> "After I finally send the message, I often feel deflated and sad. My horns have fallen off and now, like a dog with a tail between its legs, I feel I have to write well-constructed apology e-mail. It's all such a waste of time."

This syndrome could be viewed as a more extreme version of the Clark-to-Superman Effect. As in the latter case, e-mail gives an extra buffer layer to net interactions that lets some feel freer to act this way.

Advice

In general, follow the same rules of thumb suggested for the Clark-to-Superman pattern, plus the advice I gave in Chapter 6 on flaming. More specifically, try sending e-mail quoting this section of the book to the CyberHyde; realizing that s/he is exhibiting this behavior may help the person stop it.

Bitpickers: Netters Who Nitpick, Overdetail, or Overanalyze

To some folks, the online world looks like an art gallery full of crooked pictures. They forget that a gadfly can be a pest.

> "I see someone state an incorrect fact and I can't help it, I gotta correct them. People need to learn the truth."

> "Sometimes I post to a bboard for all to see the correction; other times I just respond direct to the person who made the error. Again, I just want the truth to come out—is that so wrong?"

Like many of these cyberproblems, bitpicking usually stems from the same behavior existing in one's real life. Going overboard can lead to flame wars, either about the original error, or simply about the bitpicking! This of course contributes to jamming, and in general the net suffers.

Advice

If you're a bitpicker and proud of it, here are some suggestions:

- If you must respond to netter errors, always do so by e-mailing only the "mistaken person." *Don't* post to bboards, even if that was where you first saw the error. Chances are high that others know the truth anyway; don't be a jammer *and* a bitpicker!

- Use humor in your bitpick response. It helps soften the blow, and helps avert flame wars. (Smileys may be useful here too.)

Now the flip side; when dealing with bitpickers, try these tips:

- When judging bitpicky responses, distinguish between those who truly want to help someone, and those who are just out to scorn, embarrass, or worse. If the one on the receiving end of a bitpick learns something, even if the teaching was done in a tedious way, the (potentially lifelong) beneficial result is often worth the (temporary) "inconvenience."

- If the bitpicking was done as a huge rambling rant, and this is done repeatedly, politely e-mail the bitpicker with your complaint. Stay factual, not personal; mention the need to control message size, time cost of reading them, and so on.

You can always try bitpicking a bitpicker back (try saying that ten times fast). Sometimes a taste of one's own medicine can cure. But be careful; as in all attempts at this tactic, it can backfire (with even more severe cases of the behavior you wanted to stop in someone).

Funny Fiends: Those Who Overdo Humor and How to Deal with Them

There's a wide range of opinion on what is or is not funny (or appropriate). Some netters are always in ruthless pursuit of a laugh.

> "When I hear a good joke, or think of one, I can't resist the temptation to post it on the net. I wanna share my find with the rest of the world! And since I can't seem to get on *The Tonight Show*, I use cyberspace as my outlet."

> "I know people tell me I use humor too much in my e-mail, but I just want to show my personality—loose, bohemian, and fun. By the way, have you heard this? These two trolls trudge into a bar…"

If you correspond regularly with a funny fiend, and are annoyed at their behavior, realize first that it's a free country and they are not doing anything illegal. Still, you can always get your thoughts across, in the hope they might tone down the joking with you, at least.

Advice

If you flame a "funny fiend," you're likely to trigger a flame back. Try these ideas instead:

- You can politely tell the funny person that you don't think his or her humor is appropriate for the business you are conducting over the net, or for the bboard they are using.

  For instance, posting a dirty joke to a biomed bboard would be poor cybermanners. Perhaps direct the funny fiend to another bboard, one that might be more accepting of his or her style of humor.

- Act really excited about their sense of humor and tell them you want to broadcast their jokes to all your friends, etc. Maybe this pressure of increased exposure, however sarcastic, will force the funny fiend to find funnier fodder than the frightening filler they filled your files with before.

Info Addicts: "Get Away From That Tube!" Revisited

Often the victim of this syndrome sits trading glassy stares with the computer, locked in a vague quest for miscellaneous information.

> "There's so much cool stuff online. I find myself reading bboards, one after another, and before I know it five hours have passed. I should buy stock in Visine."

> "My parents hassle me when I use the TV, but never say anything about the net. They seem to think anything on the net is good 'cause there's so much knowledge on there."

> "My friends and I are cybersurfers—we just get off on riding the bitstream waves, crisscrossing the net. We are 'riders on the cyberstorm' of information. I don't even care what I find out there—it's the journey, not the arrival, dude."

It's a safe bet that most parents, especially if they are not very computer-literate, do not restrict children's use of the net as much as other areas of their leisure time. To many (especially the computer-illiterate or -phobic), computers in general "equal" smart activities; after all, you have to be smart to use them, right?

Advice

This state of affairs may change as the net gains fame and more folks realize its positive as well as negative sides. But until then, ride on, infonauts and cybersurfers!

But wait, I hear some of you say; this book is about cybermanners—shouldn't there be rules for how often to use the net, what is too much, etc.? The fact is, this issue has not been resolved yet. Okay, here's one rule about net usage:

- As in the use of TV, film, and other leisure activities, people must decide what are acceptable limits for them. Once again, metaphors apply: thinking of net activities as another form of *leisure* can help you construct guidelines. Parents can adjust this, however, depending on the *type* of net activity being done by their children—for instance, playing an online networked game versus accessing the Library of Congress.

For you cybersurfers (and those who love and/or parent them), here are some suggestions to help achieve better navigation manners:

- If you are globetrotting via Telnet, keep *time* in mind: time zones, hour of the day, and local restrictions on computer use. For instance, avoid the heavy traffic during peak hours for whatever computer you're visiting. Also, different Telnet sites have different rules for their operations; read their info bulletins, warnings, updates, FAQs, and so on.

▥ Whenever you can, use the search program Gopher instead of Telnet or FTP to find files you want. *Gopher* (see basic Internet books again for information on how to use Gopher) lets you find net resources in a more efficient way than Telnet or FTP. The latter two methods maintain a constant link to a foreign computer so you can accomplish your search (e.g., browsing directories of files) or your file transfer. In contrast, Gopher does not need to keep a remote connection open continuously. This saves time and online resources—very good manners.

In addition, Gopher uses menus to help streamline your navigation and keep you cybersurfers "in the tube," whereas you're usually on your own with Telnet and FTP.

The Gump Effect: "Stupid Is as Stupid Does" on the Net

Believe it or not, there is a difference between stupidity and ignorance, even if the gaffes that come from them look the same.

"Life is like a box of Internet e-mail. You never know what you're gonna get."

"Stupid cybermanners is as stupid cybermanners does."

Take this last sentence (please); what does this mean? The point is: your cybermanners are only as poor *as others perceive them to be*. That is, even if you have good intentions, you can still appear insensitive, or even (shudder the phrase in this politically-correct world) dumb.

It's a fact that some netters act less knowledgeable than they really are. I call this behavior "dumbing" (others might use "the Gump Effect") because it makes a user look dumb (and, I admit, I like to invent short cute catchy names). In fact, "dumbing actions" are often born out of ignorance or laziness; I'm not implying there are a lot of dumb netters running around. For example, a newbie may not know about the wealth of FAQs (Frequently Asked Questions) available online via USENET and other net locations. Or someone may know these exist, yet not take the time to find or read them. You don't have to *be* a newbie to be *perceived* as one. Actions *do* speak loud on the net—though rarely louder than words (online actions usually *are* words).

Advice

To avoid this behavior pattern yourself:

- Always look for information on the net *before* asking the net. There are so many computers now hooked into the net, and so many methods of accessing such information, there is a very high likelihood you can find your answer online yourself.

- Unlike in the real world, there *is* such a thing as a "stupid question" on the net: one that's been answered in a FAQ. Never hurts to reiterate: get the FAQs, ma'am (and man)!

- Read this book. Hey, there's no excuse for poor cyber-manners when a book of answers already exists! But you already knew that, so tell a friend :-).

Advice for dealing with less knowledgeable netters who exhibit dumbing patterns:

- Dumbing behaviors often go away naturally. As a general principle, the net tends to correct itself. If someone asks a "dumb" question, other netters will often flame the questioner so badly that the chastened victim will take intelligent action before asking further questions. Or some other netters will be polite and, remembering how they felt when they were newbies, send information about how to get smart (like where the FAQ is and, if necessary, how to access it if it resides in a remote or hard-to-find location).

- Be empathic. Remember what it was like when you were a newbie. Was it really that long ago?

- Assume a stupid action was a mistake. That is, presume innocence rather than guilt—another (idealistic) carryover from the real world.

Robocomm: Automated Agents Online

"I am an automated reply. I am an example of what the author is talking about. I can be programmed to tell those who e-mail my master that Master is away on business, or has moved. I always say the same thing, unless a new message is programmed, in which case that will be my new verbiage. Some say I remind them of Al Gore."

I use the term *robocomm* to refer to robotic communication (or automated reply) programs. Some people use automated answering programs to answer e-mail. Many net services provide them, and their use is increasing. For example, since President Clinton is busy with his affairs (no pun intended), he uses an automated reply e-message (see the chapter on "jamming").

Will robocomm use add to the already-perceived "coldness" of the net? Perhaps, especially if it becomes as common in the future as answering machines are today. This is also true if robocomms are used too much. However, the following advice should help.

Advice

- Use robocomms when you are away or have moved. This is a clearly accepted use for them, perhaps the most popular as well. Programs such as *mailbots* (ask your system administrator how to use them properly) can help redirect your messages by telling those who e-mail you all about your new personal information if you've relocated, or your travel plans if you're vacationing. This is a great backup for e-mail forwarding (if your net service doesn't have it) or as an initial stage before forwarding (so your friends and colleagues don't keep sending to the old address).

- Don't use automated messaging in the wrong situations. For instance, if someone important to you sends e-mail, especially if it's urgent, the automated reply they get from you may be viewed as rude (however unintentional on your part). This is doubly depressing if you are not really away, and simply forgot to turn off your robocomm. So remember:

- Only turn on a robocomm when needed, and shut it off as soon as you can.
- Take care in composing the message that the robocomm will autosend. If it is overly terse, or lacks enough information for all your contacts to be satisfied, it can compound the coldness some already feel from automatic messages. Humor, as always, helps too—but keep it general, clear, and nonoffensive; you never know who may receive an autoreply from you!
- Overuse of automated messaging can jam the net. Another reason to be careful. For example, suppose you autoreply to two people, and both have set their accounts to autoreply. You can see how this can cascade to the point where many more messages are floating around than necessary (jamming has occurred).

Summary Points

- If you get e-mail from a Clark-turned-Superman, take this into account when you read and respond. If you feel you fit this pattern, it's okay as long as you don't slip into more severe harassing or flaming patterns.
- If you must respond to netter errors, always do so by e-mailing only the "mistaken person." If you bitpick, use humor. When judging bitpicky responses, distinguish between the helpful and the needlessly aggressive.
- When dealing with "funny fiends," you can politely tell the person that you don't think his or her humor is appropriate for the business you are conducting over the net, or for the bboard they are using. Or act really excited about their sense of humor, and tell them you want to broadcast their jokes to all your friends.
- Always look for information on the net *before* asking the net; unlike in the real world, there *is* such a thing as a "stupid question" on the net: one that's been answered in a FAQ.

115

- Dumbing behaviors often go away naturally; the net tends to correct itself. Be empathic. Assume a stupid action was a mistake.

- Use robocomms when you are away or have moved, but don't use automated messaging in the wrong situations. Turn it on only when needed; shut it off as soon as you can. Take care in composing the robocomm's message. Remember that overuse of automated messaging can jam the net.

part III

Going Deeper

This part of the book deals with how netters behave online with other users, and how certain behaviors could be beneficially revised if they violate the tenets of cybermanners. The first three chapters in this part deal with forging friendships online, gender issues, and a combination of the two—falling in love over the net.

And, of course, I cover cybermanners rules, violations, and advice for these new areas (which are really as old as the species).

The next four chapters deal with Rising up: institutions, ideas, ideals, and deals. "Rising up" has several meanings here. First, it refers to how, in this part of the book, we go "up" into what some might consider higher-level issues, dealing with ideas that can touch on all the scenarios discussed so far. But "rising up" also alludes to what some netters want to do, literally or virtually (using the net), which is to stop what they consider the incorrect application of such higher-level ideas (for example, the imposition of censorship and the violation of privacy rules).

chapter 9

Cybertalk and Virtual Sex: Interactive Interchange on the Net

In This Chapter

Covered topics are:

- What cybertalk is, in general
- Some rules for proper cybertalk manners
- The more specific area of virtual sex via talk channels
- Some rules for cybertalk sex

Chat Chic: Virtual Orality and Online Cybertalk

OK, I made up the terms "virtual orality" and "cybertalk"—but what good is writing a book if you can't create some new words? And they do have meaning: they both refer to the process of communicating in a real-time text-based conversation between two or more netters.

119

Presently, the Internet uses special programs such as "IRC" (Internet Relay Chat) or "talk" to accomplish cybertalk. Commercial online services have forums or conferences you can join and participate in. On the Internet, "talk" is usually reserved for two-person (one-on-one) conversation, while "chat" is used when more than two want to exchange text, but the general idea is the same. "Talk" is like a phone call, while "chat" is like a CB radio; in each case, text is transmitted instead of voices.

Net chatting is becoming the new hot thing in synchronous computer communication (as opposed to the Asynchronous mode used by e-mail and USENET). IRC allows you to talk with thousands of people around the globe, and do so on dozens of channels. Most channels focus on a specific topic, but there are no rules or restrictions on what channel topics must be.

How Cybertalk Compares to Real-world Talking

John Cook made one of the best comparisons between real discussions and the computer-based kind in an intriguing paper. He describes an experiment designed "... to assess the extent to which some traditional moral principles governing face-to-face [F2F] communication have gained acceptance by the users of computer conferences. This was done by assessing the prevailing community standards for computer conferencing on CompuServe's CB and on BITNET's Relay [both are analogs to Internet's IRC]. The assessment was carried out using... a 24-item questionnaire... for Users of 'CB's' and Other Computer 'Chats'."

The experiment found that "[t]he moral or ethical standards for computer conferencing revealed by the survey were... largely consistent with the moral principles governing [F2F] communication." However, there was one difference "suggested by the conference users' greater acceptance of practices such as adopting nicknames that are considered sexually provocative or sharing details of one's intimate personal relationships on a public channel. However, when… users were asked to evaluate the potential benefits of computer conferencing, they appeared to discount the importance of some of these practices, in a way that brought them back in line with traditional moral principles governing face-to-face communication."

This led Cook to conclude that "we do tend to attach importance to the same sort of activities both on- and off-line [and so] several traditional moral principles governing [F2F] communication have been found to be accepted by the users of computer conferences." Still, he did infer a discrepancy between on- and off-line ethical standards "in the larger range of behaviors we are willing to consider as morally acceptable in other conference users."

This implies that manners violations or questionable behaviors should find more lenience on cybertalk channels than would occur in the real world. Perhaps this is true in part because highly robust multi-user talk channels are a rather recent innovation on the net, and so are still relatively "free-form" compared to areas like e-mail and bboards. Whatever the reason for extra leniency in chat channels, this may change as the number of net users continues its steady growth; more users means more points of view, which on average might change the average opinion from lenience to intolerance. In short, the need for manners during chats should increase in the near future. In addition, there is never a good excuse for blatant manners abuses or laziness, and we should be able to find some rules to help in this regard. You guessed it—some follow immediately.

Some Manners Rules for General Cybertalk

Unless otherwise stated, I'll assume multi-person chat is the subject for the rules below (though most of the following ideas apply to two-person talk as well).

- Try to observe others before jumping in. Lurk on channels, or access stored files of chat transcripts to learn the ropes.

- Talk on others' channels before starting your own. Again, learn to walk before you run.

- Let others finish their thoughts. No one likes to be interrupted. Also, with some programs (such as "talk") it can be confusing and irritating to see text appearing on multiple parts of your screen.

- Be especially forgiving of spelling and formatting oversights. After all, we don't worry about spelling and formatting when talking in real life; worrying about such details can slow down the conversational flow. Remember that cybertalk is meant to be informal, and take place in quick bursts of ideas, as in real chatting.

- If you feel out of place on a talk "channel," switch channels. Find a new place in cyberspace. Often you can even start your own chat channel (on the Internet).

- Political correctness is revered in some circles, reviled in others. So know your audience. Don't impose PCness on an unPC area, and vice versa (unPCness on a PC area).

- Use a handle, and try using one that matches or highlights your personality. It's like wearing an outfit that shows your tastes; it can give you flair. Remember, textual appearance is the majority of how you make impressions online!

- If you detect a celeb is chatting, play it cool and remember that they're just another voice on the net. The famous are people too! And they very often feel more intimidated on the net because it's a safe bet most are new to using cyberspace. If you're a net guru, you can even become like a celeb to the celeb.

   Also, the net is like a great equalizer anyway, what with all the letters being passed back and forth being the same for all who use them.

- Don't page someone (sending the "talk" command on the Internet pages the receiver with a brief note appearing on the receiver's computer screen indicating someone wants to talk) if you know the recipient is busy. Also avoid this faux pas if the intended recipient is easily "tick-offable." (Is that a word, or did I just make it up?)

- Take all self-descriptions with a grain of salt. Make that several large grains. You must assume that some netters, for various reasons, are experimenting (or actually living day-to-day online) with false personas (pseudonyms, fake ID's, that sort of thing). Some of the reasons: they wish to try a different sex (gender) for awhile, or a new appearance, and so on. Which leads to another rule:

- Don't flame a cyberchat participant because you suspect a "false" persona is being used. After all, being able to use them is one reason some people cyberchat in the first place. And when you interact online, it is not always clear which personas are real and which are false; if you never meet F2F (face-to-face)—and most netters don't—then should "real" personas even matter? (If you're a philosopher, stop here and mull this over.)

- Don't force an F2F meeting if s/he doesn't want one. Many netters love cyberchat (either "clean" talk or sexual conversations) precisely because F2F meetings do not have to be a part of the process. Also feel free to say you want to put off an F2F decision until later; if they really like you, they'll understand.

- Refusing an F2F meeting is *not* necessarily the same as rejection. Cheer up. See the previous rule; some folks just want to keep everything virtual, even if they really like someone. Of course, it's possible that you like someone's general personality but they did one or two things you disliked; for instance, maybe they didn't exhibit good cybermanners here and there.

- As in real life, what you see or read may not be what you get. As the old saying goes, "On the Internet, no one knows you're a dog." (Or an armadillo, for that matter.) In other words, you never really know who is on the other side of that e-mail address (what their sex is, or other vital statistics). Don't feel bashful about asking questions of the sexual orientation of someone you are building a friendship or courtship with (especially if you're the type who hates the suspense of the *Saturday Night Live* "Pat" character, and must know someone's true identity and stats right away).

Or you can just revel in the ambiguity and rejoice that you can get to know someone without ever having to know their gender, age, race, or other real-world "trivialities." Besides, you might not get an answer—and even if you did, how would you know it was true?

- Don't send too many messages; like Goldilocks, try to find what is "just right." Too few messages can be viewed as lack of interest, whereas too many can be perceived as too desperate. And too too many can be interpreted as harassment.

Reach Out and Touch Some Fun: Cybersex Chat

If we apply a telephone system metaphor to online behavior, we can predict that the popularity of phone-sex numbers should carry over to a strong desire for net-based sex as well. This chapter deals with such issues related to virtual sexual relations over the Internet and other parts of the information superhighway. (I'll use the terms *virtual sex*, *cybersex*, and *cybersex chat* interchangeably, to represent the concept of having "sex" via chat channels using text interactions only; another term I like is *text sex*—partly because I invented it!) Some feel that any form of virtual sex exhibits poor cybermanners, but for those who accept the general principle, such manners questions are more complex, and we deal with them here.

One can identify several types (or levels) of interchange that occur over the net and involve sex to some degree. Some netters just want to exchange erotic images. Other people prefer to just talk *about* sex (via e-mail or bboards). To learn more about sex and sex-related issues (real and virtual) in preparation for meeting others, you should hang out in the right bboards and chat channels. An example on USENET is the soc.singles newsgroup. To achieve the next step—meeting potential mates—you should again hang out at the right bboards and chat channels. Some USENET examples include rec.nude, soc.singles, and soc.penpals.

A third class of netters, the one I concentrate on here, wants to actually participate in virtual sex, not just talk about it on bboards or via e-mail. Since I can hear you panting and getting hot out there, let's jump right in. What is online virtual sex? In a nutshell, it's a text-based version of what goes on during calls to phone-sex lines; each party says what they are feeling and/or doing to the other, who then responds in kind. Of course this can also be done by e-mail, but chat lines give *immediate feedback* the way a phone does; doing virtual sex by e-mail would be about as exciting as correspondence chess. Many devout participants claim that virtual sex can be used to bring one to a higher plane of sexual interaction. Some netters feel this is assisted by the *removal* of direct sensory touch. Of course, you can also replicate standard phone-sex fare, depending on your mood. The freedom of the net gives you a choice.

Rules for Cybersex Chat and Scoring Virtual Touch(downs)

Most of the rules for cyberchat presented above also apply to cybersex chat. However, the following (more specific) rules were compiled and condensed from various sources, including Gareth Branwyn's article on compu-sex in the book *Flame Wars*, and the FAQ for the USENET newsgroup soc.singles. Some of these rules can even be generalized and applied to cyberchatting in general.

- Type fast and write well. An anonymous computer-sex participant calls this the online "equivalent to having great legs in the real world."

- Bone up on spelling. Bad spelling is a turn-off to some, and good spelling can be a turn-*on* to others (spelling fetish, anyone?)

- Opening lines are extra important online. Why? First of all, words are all you have to make an impression (no physical cues or breathy voice to compensate or augment). Second, if you use chat channels for your cybersex, such channels can pop in and out of existence extremely fast; people can move into and out of these "rooms" just as quick. Boredom will not be tolerated in online sex, so get their attention fast and strong!

- Good navigation skills can be a turn-on, and are almost as important as good opening lines. Why? If you can find a good "compumatch" quickly, the object of your affections (Oops! I mean *person*, not object—gotta be PC, right?) may be impressed by your speed, and/or your persistence.

  Also, if you have already turned this person on and you somehow lose them (yes, switching channels *does* happen, especially with all the short attention spans today :), finding them fast will help keep them in the mood.

  You can even work this search into the courting process (i.e., the online conversation). For example, "How did you find me? I was playing hard to get by changing rooms!" "I guess I really like you." Also realize that fast navigation to where you want to go also saves you hard cash, since many compusex netters pay for online time. You can then use this saved cash to impress your compumatch during any F2F meetings that take place after your online rendezvous. (What *is* the plural of *rendezvous*, anyway?)

- Don't reveal information that is meant to be private. For example, a dialog in a private room (an area you can set up on chat channels for restricted access by you and your friends) is *confidential*. "Not even sysadmins have access to them," says Branwyn. If you have an understanding with one or more compusex "partners" to meet in a private room, don't give out its code name, since the others in your clique may assume it *is* secret. Letting the cat out of the cyberbag violates their trust (and hence, cybermanners).

- Don't assume or flaunt a sexual orientation that doesn't fit the assumed orientation of the room you're in. The more someone tries to emphasize a difference from the room's inhabitants, the ruder that person is acting. Proper cybermanners suggest that this individual change to another room that better fits his or her (or its) needs. Or he/she/it can always start a new room.

- Balance sexual "goals" (it helps to know what yours are) against the public chat manners guidelines given by your net service provider. *Public* is the key word here. Since many chat channels are public, netters hungry for more risqué sexual "action" might want to leave the public areas. Which leads to the next rule:

- If you want to interact with nonstop uninterrupted free-from-flak hot sex, take it private. You can create private rooms in the chat area of your net service; they're tailor-made for this kind of activity. As mentioned earlier, not even sysadmins are supposed to have access to such secret sanctuaries.

  Note, however, that some areas of certain service providers are so secret that their usage rules are not explained openly. In some cases, you have to figure out the right code to get to the steamy sex areas (or have someone tell you). Of course, this may actually increase the excitement (and that's a lot of what sex is about, right?), and the ultimate pleasure when you do finally enter the forbidden-hidden areas (no pun intended).

- Learn the proper "codespeak" or "cybersexese" used by other denizens of the online sex rooms. For example, there are certain codes used to tip off other users (in a public yet sexually explicit chat room) that an official person may have entered. Such an official netter is usually a *guide*—a kind of "cybercop" from the net provider that monitors rooms for proper conduct—and may either be lurking (not speaking) or even actually partaking in the sexchat.

  Some examples of code language to tip off guide presence include "Sleepy time" or "zzzzzzzz," which loosely translates to "stop talking openly about sex." Once people feel the guide is gone, someone will usually indicate this, and the frank talk resumes.

  Why would a "cybercop" matter if you are exchanging "text sex" between consenting adults? First, online services do have the option of checking around to see if their official policies are being followed. In other words,

127

know your online service's "party line" (okay, bad pun—I mean "official policy") regarding sex and chat areas, and act accordingly. If you want to bend the rules (or aren't sure you're doing so), it may be useful to know the aforementioned "tipoff cyberese" of your cyberclique. Even if you *are* doing everything right, many netters are just shy about spying by "outsiders"; the special codespeak helps here too.

- Make your room title clear enough to get its purpose and orientation across, but not so explicit that it alerts a guide/monitor. A very naughty (offensive) room title may cause a room guide to close down the room. On the flip side, a vague or misleading room title can have the same effect; for example, Branwyn relates the story of how a room named "Pictures" was once closed down because "an overzealous guide" believed that a pornographic picture exchange was going on in that room. This was not the case; computer graphics issues was the topic.

- If you want to exchange scanned images with content that may not be suitable for public consumption, use private messages or e-mail. In other words, don't do it in public (again, no sexual allusion intended).

- Don't be overly combative with a sysadmin or guide, and especially avoid arguing in a public area. If you do, you could have your membership temporarily suspended, or even permanently revoked. Think of signing on the service as getting your driver's license, and the guide as a CHiP (cop—remember that highway-patrol series?), and the net as (info) highway, and... well, you get the metaphor. You wouldn't be obnoxious to Erik Estrada, would you?

Why would someone be mad at a guide? Well, if your room was shut down for improper sexual conduct (say, sexually explicit language in a public chat area during peak day hours when official policy of your online service prohibits this), some of the more rebellious netters might be upset. You might get even madder if your conduct was fine, but incorrectly *interpreted* by a system guide or fellow user (like a jesting remark being misread or

- misquoted by one of the "humor-impaired"). But remember, two wrongs don't make a right, so don't compound a guide's error by flaming back too harshly.
- If you still have a beef with your service provider over a cybersex matter, and absolutely must "get it all out," try either a private room or e-mail. For example, using e-mail gives you time to calm down, think out your thoughts more objectively, read it over and edit, even save the file and wait overnight to make sure it's the proper tone.
- It's perfectly acceptable to "swing" online even if you're monogamous in the real world. After all, this fantasy element—being able to do online what some feel they can't do for real—is one of the main attractions of cybersex. And, of course, cybersex is safe, though I wouldn't be surprised if some hacker concocts a digital condom. Perhaps to protect against a computer virus :-)
- But if cybersex rooms are used with the goal of cheating for real at a later time, you're crossing over into poor cybermanners (to say the least). Even if the rooms were only used to set up such trysts, this is getting into the realm of bad taste, and getting out of the spirit of cybersex. Of course, all this should be biased by your point of view and that of your virtual partner.
- When partaking in multi-person fantasy interactions, make the effort to maintain eroticism and consistency. That is, keep everyone in the mood, and don't ruin things by popping the "fantasy bubble." An example: if man X says he's standing up, don't make an action that assumes he is sitting. Such events in effect shout "contradiction!," and may jar some of the participants, reminding them this is all just happening over phone lines with text-based personas!
- And, most important of all, don't whine and complain that cybersex chat is not really sex, or something along those lines. You're being a party pooper, and you'll get flamed royally as well!
- In general, follow the rules and play the part for the area you are having cybersex interactions in. For example, if

you're reading or posting to the USENET group rec.nude, it is generally assumed that you are buck naked. Some claim it's mandatory or you can get kicked off the group. Of course, you may wonder why this matters, when no one could prove whether you're really nude. But you should at least *act* as if you're nude; play the part that is considered apropos to the area you are in, whether it's a newsgroup or a chat room.

Q & A on Cyberdating and Net Love

Here's a sampling of questions and answers to help guide you in using the USENET soc.singles newsgroup—and other newsgroups—to find a "compumate" (some of these items are derived from the soc.singles FAQ):

Q: Should I post personals ads on soc.singles?

No. Personal ads belong in the alt.personals groups; there are even groups for people with specific tastes (like alt.personals.poly, or alt.personals.bondage). If you want to post a request for pen-friends rather than a personal ad, there's also soc.penpals which is dedicated for just that very thing. Do not post personals in soc.singles; you will annoy the readership and not get any positive responses.

Q: If I'm not supposed to post personals, what kinds of articles should I post?

Think of soc.singles as an electronic hybrid of a cocktail party and a soap opera. Appropriate posts should be both interactive and entertaining—that is, their content should both invite the participation of others in the electronic conversation and be entertaining to its readers. You might pose an open question to the readership about some aspect of the human condition as it applies to singleness, or you might reply to another contributor's post and add an observation that sheds light on a different aspect of the issue under discussion. Personal ads are a good example of what sort of posting isn't appropriate because they are neither of these—they aren't conducive to public discussion, nor (for most people) are they entertaining.

Q: Do I have to be single to post on soc.singles?

No. The only requirement is that you have *been* single at some time in your life, know someone who is or was, or are interested in some of the subjects that people meeting either of these conditions have been known to talk about. (Pretty exclusive group, right?)

Q: Is there anything besides personal ads that should be avoided?

Of course there are things that are best avoided—perhaps the most important of these are emotional issues for which other newsgroups have been created. Topics like abortion, politics, religion, and other such things are best avoided, not because they aren't valid issues, but because, like personal ads, it's too easy for them to take over the newsgroup and drive off those of us who participate on soc.singles because we like soc.singles. Remember, anyone who wants to debate abortion can go to talk.abortion and anyone who wants to post and read personals can go to alt.personals*—but if soc.singles gets turned into soc.talk.alt.personals.abortion.religion.politics, there's no newsgroup where the soc.singlers can go to continue their discussions.

Q: Just what does "single" mean anyway?

In the context of soc.singles, it means "unmarried"; there's a tendency for "singles' issues" being discussed on soc.singles to be directed towards people who don't currently have a long-term committed partner, but anything interesting and/or important to people who aren't married is appropriate.

Summary Points

The highlights of general cyberchat advice:

- Try to observe others before jumping in, and talk on others' channels before starting your own.
- Let others finish their thoughts.
- Be forgiving of spelling and formatting oversights.

- If you feel out of place on a talk "channel," switch channels—and don't impose PCness on an unPC area, or vice versa.
- Take all self-descriptions with a grain of salt.
- Don't force an F2F (face-to-face) meeting if s/he doesn't want one, and remember that refusing an F2F meeting is *not* necessarily the same as rejection.
- As in real life, what you see or read may not be what you get.

Now, regarding cybersex, here are the main rules of advice (I know, you're so busy on those sex channels you don't have time to read the main section):

- Opening lines are extra important online.
- Don't reveal information that is meant to be private.
- Balance sexual "goals" against the public-chat-manners guidelines given by your net service provider. If you want to chat nonstop uninterrupted free-from-flak hot sex, take it private.
- Learn the proper "codespeak" and sexual orientation of the online sex rooms you participate in.
- If you want to exchange scanned images with content that may not be suitable for public consumption, use private messages or e-mail.

chapter 10

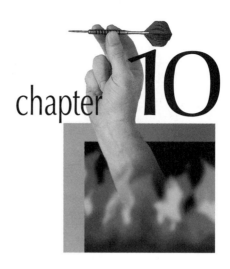

Gender Issues in Cyberspace

In This Chapter

This chapter focuses on providing:

▌▎ Advantages women feel cyberspace communication gives them, as compared to the real world.

▌▎ Assorted advice on online gender issues.

Many believe the battle of the sexes still rages online. Some believe men and women act the same way they do in real life when they interact in the cyberspace realm; others claim people behave worse. For example, there is anecdotal evidence that some men who are shy in real life don long-suppressed, overly aggressive alter-egos when interacting virtually.

One thing is certain: there is mounting evidence that men and women communicate differently in cyberspace, and concentrate on different issues when exploring the net.

Advantages of Cyberspace (Versus Real-life) Communication for Women

Millions of men and women are discovering the brave new world of the Internet, but women in particular are finding certain opportunities that are less common in the "real" world. The following examples are not scientifically proven (or even unscientifically concocted), but rather are culled from *some* opinions that *some* women have made public. Note that these can apply to anyone, but women especially have noted that they address some of the elements lacking in real-world communication.

- Less chance of interruption or censorship. Some females have commented that interruptions seem to happen more often in real life than online. E-mail and bboard messages stand on their own and cannot be interrupted. They can be argued about and deleted, but they are "alive"—in intact form—for at least some amount of time. And, in general, bboards do not censor messages on the basis of the writer's gender. If they did, those censored would just change their online sex (which I hear happens a lot anyway).

- A more even playing field. Words look the same whether a man or woman sends them. Online personas (or "handles," to borrow from CB terminology) can be gender-neutral if one prefers—in other words, in some circumstances gender can become a non-issue online. And the lack of the normal variety of emotional nuance (for example, no real yelling is possible other than THIS VARIETY—wow, intimidating, huh?) and visual/aural stimulation (body language, physical attractions, etc.) tends to make netters focus more on issues and ideas rather than on surface superficialities. (Some women in particular relish the chance to have meaningful discussions where men must "stare at their brain" rather than other parts of their anatomy.)

- More support for voicing opinions. For one thing, you can find a lot of people to back up an opinion when millions are reading individual posts or on-going discussions on

USENET. This gives you a greater feeling of security when jumping into a discussion, especially for newbies who are a bit daunted by the whole process.

▮ More opportunities to foster such support, such as through chat channels and bboards that are "for ladies only."

Now, I am not saying that *everything* is perfect for women online; there are certainly examples of poor male cybermanners toward females. For example, *Newsweek* reported how one woman was flamed for sharing her thoughts over a male-dominated *Star Trek* discussion bboard. One cannot simply blame the net for causing this behavior; it can happen just as easily in the real world. Even so, the nature of the net often allows women to avoid gender-related communication problems; net-based interaction often leads to better manners toward women—expressed as good cybermanners—than would be found in other media or in real-world contexts.

Advice Regarding Online Gender Issues

▮ Don't send e-mail just because of someone's online sexual persona; it's tacky and can be viewed as harassment. In other words, just don't do it. One woman in particular told me about how men flood her e-mailbox with e-letters just because she has a female "handle" online.

And besides: names can be phony. Wouldn't you feel stupid wasting time on a person of a sex you're not interested in? Remember the famous saying regarding Internet personas: on the net, no one knows you're a dog (or, for that matter, a seal). So don't bark up the wrong tree!

▮ Don't harass someone online if you wouldn't in real life. In other words, don't do it, period. Sounds like an obvious rule, but some people must constantly be reminded that views and interpretations made online often mirror those of the real world. Just because harassment occurs in a virtual world doesn't mean the feelings of those who ENTER that world are any less real.

Chapter 10

- Basing assumptions about someone's net expertise on gender is PI (and can be grossly inaccurate). Sometimes such assumptions are based on one's own experience, but carrying such views over when meeting new people on the net can make a terrible first impression—and even deliver a virtual slap in the face. Not a recommended route to online conviviality.

- If you're not sure of someone's true gender, and want/prefer/need to know, try checking their publicly available information. For example, many netters complete what is called a *plan file* (also referred to simply as a *.plan* or *plan*), in which more details are provided about the person who owns that file (usually full name, affiliation, interests, and often real-world address and phone information). The main use for plan files is to give other netters a chance to find out more about you without your having to answer introductory or investigative queries all day (there is enough jamming on the net already, as you read earlier).

  Consulting plan files can sometimes give you enough information to detect gender, but not always. For one thing, what if the plan's written by someone like that *Saturday Night Live* character Pat, who loves to maintain androgyny at all costs? Numerous netters do too. Also, people can lie, I'm afraid to say—though such poor cybermanners can get you kicked off some services. In short, don't assume plans will always give you a final answer, but do use them at least as partial evidence.

- Don't be bashful about trying new online personas. It is, after all, part of the appeal of the net that one can, for instance, "try on" a new gender and see how it feels. The online realm gives everyone the opportunity to see how the other shoe fits—and this applies not only to changing gender, but age, race, nationality, or any other characteristic that cannot be detected easily in cyberspace. Perhaps this ability to experiment with identity and points of view will not only lead to better cybermanners online, but rub off in "real reality" as well.

Q & A

Q: I heard someone developed an online relationship with a 12-year-old of the opposite sex. Isn't that terrible cybermanners at the least, abuse at worst?

This is a very delicate issue. This example actually occurred, and no less an authority than advice columnist Ann Landers supported the "defense of the computer junkie" that there is often no way to determine the gender or age or other characteristics that people can easily detect in other forms of interaction. As Landers points out, "strangers always put on their best face when they are trying to make a good impression," and this applies just as much to cyberspace. In fact, it is often easier on the net because there are little or no extra cues to contradict the words of an expert conversationalist. Typer beware!

Q: How can I tell who is lying and who is telling the truth when describing themselves online? There seem to be an awful lot of doubles for Claudia Shiffer and Mel Gibson inhabiting the net.

Unfortunately you can't tell, and there will always be a lot of liars out there. As the net technology matures, and voice as well as video elements are added, it might become harder to present false personas. Maturing technology, however, is often a double-edged sword; in this case, it might make it *easier* to misrepresent yourself. For example, there are home-security devices that can disguise a woman's voice as a man's; Laurie Anderson did a good job of it on some of her records, using 1985 technology. And if such toys as wave-form editing and "video toasters" get into the online act, we're back where we started. As on *Jeopardy*, there are no easy answers.

Q: There already exists an online club for men only. Should such clubs exist? Have any proved useful for their members?

Freedom of speech rears its head again; online clubs do have a right to exist. They are often useful for bonding between people, particularly those who may feel too shy or constrained by social customs to do so in the real world.

Will there be future battles where women try to force entry into men-only virtual clubs, or vice versa? It may be a moot point, since it is easy for one sex to masquerade as another in cyberspace.

Q: Can there be an online equivalent of rape? How can one identify this, and what should be done in response?

A hypothetical situation: suppose two people are on a chat channel, perhaps doing cybersex activities, or even just "regular" talk. If one party starts to "do actions" (that is, say things that represent the action) that indicate sexual advances, and if the other party does not want this, and indicates this fact, then we have the beginning of a "virtual rape" situation. As long as one can get off a chat channel, however, there should be no chance of its completion. And there is always the sysadmin or a guide one can contact for help.

The problem is tracking down those who start these scenarios (the "rapists"); they can be under false or anonymous names. The future of online tracking mechanisms may affect this situation; for now, the best course for "victims" might be to switch to systems like eWorld, which are requiring real names online (no fake IDs).

Summary Points

Some rules of advice on gender matters:

- Don't send e-mail just because of someone's online sexual persona; it's tacky and can be viewed as harassment.
- Don't harass someone online if you wouldn't in real life (in other words, don't do it).
- Assumptions about someone's net expertise based on sex are PI.
- If you're not sure of someone's true gender, and want/prefer/need to know, try checking their publicly available information.
- Don't be bashful about trying new online personas.

chapter 11

Making Friends and Fostering Community in Cyberspace

In This Chapter

There are right and wrong ways to meet people online. Here we discuss them, looking at behaviors that will help folks meet, keep people your friends, and avoid actions that will push people away. I will codify these thoughts into rules of proper conduct—for finding friends, maintaining them, and fostering community.

Also covered: why (and how) groups congregate online—for both expected and unexpected reasons—and the types of communities that form over the net.

Background

Why do people try to meet people over the net? There are many reasons, including...

- ▓ You want to find new folks who share your interests (especially if you are not succeeding too well at this in the real world).

- You want to find folks with new interests you want to learn about.
- Cultural curiosity. You may want to see how people around the country or world think, what their opinions on a topic are. Sometimes people in the same area seem to think alike on certain issues, and new views can be invaluable in many ways.
- You are a professional, looking for new colleagues to exchange ideas with.
- You want to set the stage for more intimate interactions. (See Chapter 9 for more on virtual sex, cyberdating, and net love.)
- You are a member of a specific community that could use a net forum to increase awareness, share experiences, or expand participation.

Internet expert Michael Strangelove points out that "[u]ntil roughly three years ago, Internet culture was largely rooted in the scientific, academic, military and technical realms of the Western nations… [b]ut the vast majority of Internet growth has occurred in the past two years, resulting in an explosion of a great diversity of user groups." Many of these groups want to share unique experiences, both within the community and with those outside of it. Groups often want to expand and recruit new members as well. The net is a wonderful tool for achieving these goals.

In fact, Strangelove points out that "[o]ne of the earliest and most active users of computer networks is the Native American community. A people with a strong sense of community which have been marginalized by society have found that the Internet is a means to maintain a distinct identity and foster community across vast distances. This should stand as an indication of what the Internet is all about: not high tech and hot machines, but communication, community, and identity."

Advice for Finding Friends Online

- Hang out in virtual coffeehouses online. On the USENET, there are several—virtual hangouts like alt.pub.dragons-inn and alt.pub.cloven-shield or alt.pub.havens-rest. None of these pubs cater to those wishing to just rap about the real world, but alt.pub.coffee-house.amethyst does. Its rules (no fictional personas, no role-playing, no alcohol) help focus the discussions to more honest and down-to-earth topics, which in turn makes meeting new friends online and really getting to know them an easier pursuit. Also, these rules make a good example for use in the new online gathering spots that will undoubtedly surface (and do so at an ever-increasing rate as the net population balloons).

- Treat others in cyberspace as you'd want them to treat you. (Okay, I snuck in the Golden Rule again. Just wanted to show how ubiquitous it is.)

- Meet others in soc.penpals USENET bboard. R U Desperately seeking? Are U an SF (single female) wanting to meet an SM (single male)? Then the soc.penpals bboard is for you. This newsgroup exists to help netters meet. Some of the meetings spin off to other media, such as real penpal letters using snail-mail.

Advice for Fostering Community Online

- Start a bboard for your community—those who want to learn more about it, or those who actively participate in it. When there are enough like-minded people in your "group mind," a new bboard can help solidify the group, as well as attract even more like-minded folk.

- Have regular chats online. This can serve as a precursor or adjunct to a community bboard, or as follow-up to initial conversations you have over e-mail. Also more immediate and interactive than bboards or e-mail.

- Meet off-line. There is no reason relationships spawned on the net need to stay restricted to the virtual realm. And e-mail is perfect for scheduling real-world meetings, too.

- Keep a mailing list of people in your community that you regularly send e-mail to. Again, this can act as precursor or adjunct to community bboards or e-mail.

Summary Points

Many reasons exist for meeting new people over the net; some of the most common include the desire to find like-minded folks with shared interests or new ones, new professional colleagues, people you'd like intimate interactions with, or members (current or new) of a specific community. As net usage grows, and more groups discover its power for finding and linking members, even more real-world communities should develop "second homes" online.

The main rules for finding friends via the net:

- Hang out in virtual coffeehouses online. (Maybe some serve virtual Starbuck's.)

- Treat others in cyberspace as you'd want them to treat you.

- Meet others in the soc.penpals USENET bboard.

The main rules for fostering community via the net:

- Start a bboard for your community.

- Have regular chats online.

- Meet off-line.

- Keep a mailing list of people in your community that you regularly send e-mail to.

chapter 12

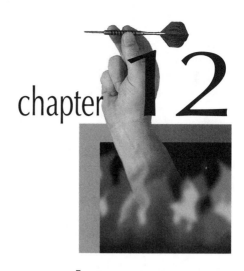

Net Privacy and Account Protection

Background

George Carlin made fun of the words you couldn't say on television. Currently the net is not as censored, but as more everyday folk "tune in" to cyberspace, and as the possibility of corporate sponsors looms in the future, issues arise:

- Will freedoms that are taken for granted today continue?
- What is encryption, and why is it such a hot net issue today?
- If encryption catches on, when will it be useful, and when will it be inappropriate? (Can courtesy and secrecy coexist?)
- Who should have access to your messages at work, either business-related or personal?
- Should personal messages be allowed at work, or should companies have the freedom to restrict such practices (as they sometimes do with personal phone calls)?
- Should online services be allowed to censor any messages on their system, like PRODIGY did in the recent past

(which resulted in a barrage of angry flames, and led many members to jump ship and sign on with other services)?

Then there is the whole issue of online/virtual sex discussed earlier. Is it insignificant that, as of December 5, 1993, the most popular USENET newsgroup in the world (when the groups were ordered by traffic volume) was alt.binaries.pictures.erotica, with an estimated 280,000 readers worldwide and recent traffic of roughly 24 megabytes per month? Then there is the recent case (July 1994)—reported on Public Radio—of a Lawrence Livermore Lab computer being used to store sexual material online. These and other facts and events bring up several questions, such as: Should online sexual activity of any kind be allowed? Given such user momentum, is complete sexual censorship even possible? Assuming it is not, what cybermanners should apply to the storage, transmission, and use of sexually explicit cybercontent?

We cannot answer all these questions here, but will give you a flavor of the issues involved.

Examples and Anecdotes: Privacy Matters

You can say that again. It does matter—to millions of netters.

For example, famous people often try to keep their e-mail addresses private, so they don't get flooded with e-mail (see the "jamming" section). Movie critic Roger Ebert: "An e-mail address is... a private thing." He feels that books that make e-mail addresses public should not be published. Novelist Tom Clancy agrees, asking that writers not publish his e-mail address. Clancy is one of many netters who use e-mail mainly for business; in *Fortune* he stated that "If I get deluged [with e-mail]... I can't do that anymore"; he expresses the hope that people will "agree that even authors can have privacy."

Another reason privacy is important to consider: e-mail can surface (or resurface, if it's old) in original, revised, or edited form—appearing where and when you least expect it. Do you really want very explicit or confidential love letters (or other sensitive information) lying around exposed on someone's virtual desk—especially if the one it lands on belongs to your boss?

Plus, did you know that businesses routinely monitor employees' e-mail, and that there are no current restrictions on their doing so? In fact, there are cases of companies hiring outside companies to resurrect "dead" e-mail—or other files which were deleted but not fully erased. (Would George Orwell be pleased to know that the issues he addressed in his novel *1984* are alive and well—or at least undead? Perhaps his first draft was actually called *1994*.)

Such incidents are more common than we'd like to admit in the Electronic Wild West. It's a safe and sane policy *never to commit anything to e-mail that would shame you if it turns up later in the staff newsletter*. While e-mail poses as an ephemeral and informal medium, easy printing and forwarding of digital mail may lend it a permanence and reader circulation that was never intended, and which can never be lived down.

So, if a person has something confidential to communicate, they should consider using the telephone or setting up a meeting. And for goodness sake, if we must gossip, let's at least have the decency to do it in the time-honored, truly graphical, real-time-animated, face-to-face, homo-sapien way that leaves no evidence behind.

Some Rules for Enhancing Your Online Privacy and Protection

- Change your password as often as your memory can handle. Many newbies use passwords that may be easy for hackers to crack (or bad guys in general to access)—for instance, Doug Doofus using the password "dougd" or "ddoofus." The best passwords are truly off-the-wall, hopefully a combination of two short *unrelated* words, and perhaps some numbers thrown in. And something you can remember (something memorable to you *and only* you) is also preferred.

For example, my password is—OOPS! That reminds me of another rule:

- *Don't give out your password*, or other key account information. Duh!
- Be careful on the cc: line in your messages. So often overlooked, this is one of the simplest and easiest ways to ensure your privacy. For example, this is important if you only want certain people to get your e-mail ("for certain eyes only").

  Internet expert, writer, and publisher Michael Strangelove relates an incident relevant here: "A competing publisher… once sent a note to all his editors warning them not to talk to me, as he saw me as potential competition on a number of products. Quite by mistake, he included my name in the list of recipients, so I also received the internal e-memo. I messaged everyone back explaining that there was no need to fear me. The publisher apologized and that was the end of the matter. Was rather funny at the time…"

- Use a blind cc: (or bcc:) to send copies of messages to people when the sender or receiver wants this copy to be a secret. For example, a message receiver might not want his/her e-mail address to be generally known to just anybody (a *receiver-privacy* choice); respect this preference, and assume it holds unless told otherwise. Or this receiver might not want everyone to know that Jack S is sending him/her a copy of the message. Or, the sender might not want everyone to know that Jill R is getting a copy of the message (a *sender-privacy* choice).

- To increase privacy, leave behind as little evidence as possible. In this case, "evidence" means files, data, and so on that can reveal a lot about the person or persons involved.

This rule leads to more specific variations, such as: when you delete a file (e-mail or otherwise), use a program that actually erases the file completely. (Software that will do this is readily available for your personal computer; Internet versions of programs that do true erasing may be harder to track down.) On your PC, a "normal" delete operation just removes the tag that points to a file. Hence the file can be recovered with file-recovery software and other techniques. A periodic "true-erase" sweep should suffice to maintain privacy; if you lean toward the paranoid persuasion, erase every time. (Some companies also enable you to reset the default delete operation into a full erase.)

For your online account, check to see whether deleted files go to a different location (deleted mail sometimes gets put in a special mailbox). If so, delete the file(s) from the new location. For software that will do this, check your online service provider or your local PC store.

- Consider encrypting your messages. This can help fight off the privacy infringements that occur when, for example, employers monitor your e-mail. Encryption methods are becoming more commonplace everywhere, and methods are more widely available, in a wider variety.

  If you decide to use encryption to ensure privacy, or at least increase its chances, make sure the receiver knows how to decode (or decrypt) your message. Otherwise it'll all be Greek to the geek (er, I mean, the nice person on the other end).

- Weigh the safety of security measures against the purpose and image of your system/network. Some systems *are* meant for public access, so the chance of hackers getting in and doing damage is not large enough to justify an image that may keep good users away, or simply keep good guys out by making it too hard to enter the system. And if everyone will just get along (and get this book), there will be peace and love everywhere anyway—so don't worry.

Summary Points

In general, you should consider privacy matters for those activities or pieces of data that you feel most vulnerable letting others know about. Don't go overboard, however; weigh the potential benefits against your likely costs (the time, effort, and worry involved). More specifically, here are some brief summary rules of thumb (your "private" short list):

- Change your password as often as your memory can handle.

- Don't give out your password, or other key account information.

- Be careful on the cc: line in your messages

- Use a blind cc: (or bcc:) to send copies of messages to people when sender or receiver wants this copy to be a secret.

- To increase privacy, leave behind as little evidence as possible.

- Consider encrypting your messages.

- Make the problem required to break your security too hard to solve.

- Weigh the safety of security measures against the purpose and image of your system/network.

chapter

Virtual Ventures: Working, Advertising, and Profiting Online

In This Chapter

Although its roots are in nonprofit endeavors, the Internet now has about half its traffic taken up by business enterprise; we are fast approaching the day when commercial netters will outnumber the "old guard" (researchers and educational users). Business-related traffic is, by some estimates, the fastest growing area of the net; other estimates claim its size is doubling each year.

This chapter will cover cybermanners for three aspects of doing business on the net: using the net properly at work (whatever that may be), advertising over the net (or "cybertising"), and pursuing cyberprofits and success in your online cyberventures.

Chapter 13

Cybermanners Related to Your Work Life

Advice

- Check your e-mail every day, especially in the morning.

  You can't use "I'm a newbie!" as an excuse for not learning how to check your e-mail; if you get messages that sit on your account unread, you could not only be making the senders mad, you could be missing out on vital information (such as a meeting you must attend). In addition, unread e-mail adds to virtual clutter in your computer files and can bog down the company system.

  Morning e-mail checks ensure that you note any new meetings or schedule changes before it's too late. (Afternoon checks are good to break up your post-lunch nap.)

- Don't send e-mail over the heads of people you should be talking to. For instance, going over your boss's head to e-mail your boss's boss is a virtual (as well as a real) faux pas.

- Don't "do" personal e-mail on company time. Sending romantic e-mail to the boss's daughter during work hours would be another netter no-no.

  Once again, in the two previous rules, we see how applying rules from real life to your virtual one is almost always a good idea, at least as a starting point for good cybermanners.

- If you send a message containing some of your opinions (or are just plain paranoid), use a disclaimer stating that they are your views and not necessarily your employer's.

  This boils down to business common sense. Companies don't want employees seeming to represent them when they don't. Unfortunately, net messages (as we've discussed throughout this book) can easily be misinterpreted, so disclaimers are the safest way to avoid potential problems. Usually disclaimers are put somewhere in the sig. And they can often be quite funny. Some examples:

Disclaimer: The views expressed above are not necessarily those of my employer. In fact, my employer may not even have views. (I'm not at liberty to say, at this time.)

Disclaimer: The views in this message are my own, not those of any other being in the known universe.

Disclaimer: Mr. X's views are those of Mr. X alone. I'm not sure about Mr. Ed.

Disclaimer: This was written for me. I hate it. So was that.

Disclaimer: I take no responsibility for the above message; read at your own risk. I also take no responsibility for this disclaimer. I also take no prisoners.

Disclaimer: Mie speling is nun of yur bizniss, so doo knot flaam mee.

Disclaimer: This disclaimer absolves Zig Zyzzy from any guilt for anything, real or imagined, past or future. I hope this covers everything.

Disclaimer: This disclaimer sucks. But I'm not responsible (for this disclaimer; I am, however, a responsible citizen of cyberspace).

Examples like this last disclaimer are useful because not only are they funny (well, at least I tried), they're so layered it would take years in court to figure out, which should also help shield you from any flak.

If you're *really* scared, use *all* of the above (but don't blame me if you get a virtual satchel of sig flames).

- Learn the accepted rules and codes of conduct for each bboard you intend to place ads on.
- If you have an academic or nonprofit-business account, it is probably best to avoid business-related (profit-making) activity over your net connection.

Ask your local Internet provider or system administrator or online postmaster if you are not sure about local authorized use policy. *FreeNets* (online service providers) that have little or no cost for users) often have similar restrictions.

Manners Rules for Net Advertising and Commercial Success

New online users with money-making goals often ask, "How can I sell information (like an online journal) over the net? Isn't information free?" A famous net saying is that "information wants to be free," but that doesn't mean it always is! Sometimes the way it's packaged makes the difference. The rules that follow are derived mainly from Michael Strangelove's advice on a specific side of net business: *Internet advertising* (an area I call "cybertising"). The final few rules also encapsulate his general advice for helping a commercial venture succeed online:

▋ Find out what is acceptable.

Within some Internet bboards, any commercial activity, no matter how subtle, is unacceptable and will be met with a strong negative response (usually called "flaming"). Take the time to "listen in" to the bboard to which you intend to post. Notice what other people post, and what the group's reaction is to commercial messages. If a press release or product announcement is met with intense flaming, then do not risk alienating this group of Internet users with your commercial message.

▋ Post only to appropriate bboards.

Begin your market research by identifying the appropriate bboards—which may, depending on where you do business on the net, be called *conferences, forums, lists,* or *newsgroups.* If you are selling purebred dogs, for example, do not post your message to the cat lover's list. Some bboards have FAQ files (Frequently Asked Questions); read them to determine the nature of the discussions and acceptable use policies. Also, be careful with bboards that have similar names. For instance, posting résumés is okay on misc.jobs.resumes, but not on misc.jobs.offered.

- Keep it short.

  If you suspect brevity to be the soul of many things in this book, you're correct!

  Avoid sending long e-mail messages or bboard v-ads. Your product or service announcements should never exceed two screens in length (about 50 lines long); *one screen*—less than 25 lines—is even better cybermanners (and the preferable default). Many individuals on the Internet receive a considerable amount of e-mail, so your message must be short and to the point if it is going to be read at all. You can note in your posting that further details are available upon request.

- Avoid sensationalism.

  The Internet community is content-oriented, whereas most advertisers deal in style, metaphor, image, and hype. Traditional advertising copy will not go over well on the net. The Internet community appreciates quality, filtered information, so find a way to add value to your message.

  Give something of value, and you'll receive interest (pun intended) from others on the net. Couch your message in commentary on industry trends, create an electronic newsletter that provides a range of related information, enter into dialogue with bboard users about surrounding issues. Remember that nothing is more obvious in simple "low-tech" text messages than empty hype.

- Create your own bboard, especially if you prefer passive cybertising.

  For example, it is possible to create a USENET newsgroup for discussion of your products (USENET is received by most Internet users, and contains over six thousand newsgroups). Many companies have already done so (ZEOS, for example, has several newsgroups, such as biz.zeos.general). This is a form of passive Internet-facilitated marketing. Passive advertising on the net allows a business to create a forum for dialogue, and invite the rest of the Internet to join in. By creating your own bboard, moderating the submissions (filtering out irrelevant postings), and providing high-quality information—not only about your products but about your particular commercial sector—you will establish a growing readership in much the same way a newsstand magazine does.

▮▮ Interact with the Internet community.

For the immediate future, the primary focus of Internet-facilitated advertising will not be expensive visual productions (at least until the domination of Mosaic and similar tools), but rather, the dialogues with desired market areas found in *thousands* of discussion groups. Given this state of affairs, the business world is going to have to learn a new language when it communicates to the net community—the language of content-based, interactive, community-oriented dialog. Unidirectional pontificating from corporate sales and marketing offices will only alienate the typical Internet user.

To be fully accepted by the majority of netters, a business will need to understand and participate in the virtual communities they wish to reach. Hence business must be willing and prepared to converse in an appropriate manner, on the appropriate bboards. Unlike any other medium familiar to advertisers, the net is fully bi-directional—so be prepared to answer for your product or service if it is less than 100% satisfactory. The net user will not hesitate to tell you otherwise, as well as tell the rest of the Internet community! These factors make assimilation into net culture quite analogous to expansion into a foreign country—and just as much care must be taken in this new virtual land. The pressure is truly on, net venturists!

▮▮ Most advertisers will probably fail at their initial attempt at Internet-facilitated advertising.

Why will many advertisers fail (especially older, more traditional ones) when they succumb to the seduction of the virgin fields of the Internet? Because this virtual community is oriented towards content. In contrast, advertisers in other media usually focus on image and style—broad archetypes delivered to mass audiences. But the language of the Internet, for the majority of its population, and for some time to come, is "low ASCII"—(that is, text containing Aa through Zz and 1 through 9, plus a few miscellaneous characters).

More than being a mainly text-based environment, the Internet is first and foremost an oral culture, where the keyboard mediates the spoken word to a complex matrix of subcultures, among millions of users. The ability to understand, act, and react with sensitivity to evolving net culture should foster success for any business entering into this global matrix. Be forewarned—the Internet is not television, not the Post Office, not newspapers; it's a hybrid of all these and more, hence business must adapt to it, not vice versa.

- The Internet does not guarantee a hot market or easy money. Mass markets don't yet exist online.

Restrictions on business use of the net are being phased out. This does not mean, however, that the net is automatically becoming as hot a market as its hype claims. Internet business expert Michael Strangelove predicts that "[f]or quite some time to come, the Internet will never represent a mass market such as TV where content is controlled and packaged to a limited number of pre-defined and demographically homogenous audiences consisting of millions of viewers." In other words, the overall net will likely stay semi-chaotic for a while longer; smaller virtual villages will probably form and grow in a stable fashion within this global dynamic fabric.

- Wake-up call to net-based businesses: "When in Virtual Rome, do as the Virtual Romans do."

Virtual communities are gathered into thousands of discussion areas whose sizes range from hundreds to thousands of participants, but there are no uniform groups of millions. *The challenge of the Internet-facilitated business is to find a way to reach these virtual communities on their terms, respecting their local customs.* The Internet is very big, but it is not a mass market that can be easily reached through mass mailing. Avoid mass mailings! Remember the backlash the lawyers Canter and Siegel received when they "spammed the net" in a mass ad flood? Take heed and avoid greed.

Q & A

Q: Should I put my e-mail address on my business card, or will others tell me I'm a geek as their eyes glaze over?

Put it on if you want to get e-mail, just as you put phone numbers on there if you want calls. Also, the subliminal message of putting it on is useful—telling people who are *not* online yet to get their butts to the net already, so we can all communicate easier and faster!

Q: Can I use humor when dealing with professional business types online?

It's an option, but make sure the humor used is appropriate to the type of people you're dealing with. For example, you wouldn't want to throw in dirty jokes when sending a message to several board chairmen—but less risqué humor, in context with the business matters you are discussing, should be fine.

Q: Is it OK for a "little guy" like me to post an ad on the net— even if I'm not using the net for daily business? If so, where and how is it best to do so?

Anyone can at least *try* to post an ad, but if you put it in the wrong place you could get flamed—or, worse, bumped off the net. The example of Canter and Siegel showed what can happen when someone tries a mass mailing ad (spamming); they reached a lot of potential customers, all right, but most were offended, and their volume of flame mail forced the advertisers off the net for awhile. But hey, at least they're famous now, right? :-)

Where to post ads: in the proper bboard. Use bboard topic titles to help you, but not too far; read the FAQ for that bboard to be sure. (One reason Canter and Siegel got so much flak was that there *aren't* thousands—or even hundreds—of bboards that deal with getting a green card. This was the primary focus of their ad offering legal assistance, yet they posted to all those irrelevant bboards anyway.) Try to limit your post to one or two discussion groups. Lurk on the boards to confirm your hunch about which is the best place to advertise. But keep in mind: some netters have passionate feelings about commercialization of the net, and hence may dislike you for running an ad at all.

Q: So what's the best way to run an ad?

Give something of value in your post, something netters can learn that goes beyond just your pitch. Disguise it as entertaining and fun. Use lots of humor. In general, use the same techniques the TV ads and MTV use. No, that *doesn't* mean lie. ;-)

Q: If unsolicited net advertising is permitted, why is it frowned upon by so many people?

Unsolicited advertising is a gray area of Internet culture, and therefore requires very careful planning and execution to avoid the wrath of an extremely vocal community. There is no one to tell you *not* to send unsolicited commercial e-mail on the Internet, but if you send out 10,000 annoying advertisements, you may get deluged with 10,000 complaints. (Many netters consider unsolicited net ads to be analogous to telemarketers calling them at dinnertime—especially if this is done by e-mail.) Companies who disregard Internet users' wishes are likely to find that the Internet community has a long memory (as any "oral" culture does) and is quite capable of engaging in anti-advertising campaigns and boycotts. What company would want such a negative image?

Q: Can I send an E-Ad to every Internet user I can find e-mail addresses for?

Some overzealous folks might even ask whether it is possible to send an electronic mail advertisement (E-Ad) to *every* user on the Internet. Fortunately for the Internet, it is not possible to send an E-Ad to every person on the Internet. Unfortunately for the Internet, it is probably only a matter of time before someone figures out a method of doing so. However, huge e-mail lists can still be used to send "junk e-mail" to many non-interested netters. Since our government has created laws to deal with junk faxes, it's a natural extension of this concept to consider junk e-mail poor manners too.

Summary Points

Some general job-related cybermanners rules:

- To keep in touch and informed, check e-mail every day.
- Don't send e-mail over the heads of people you should be talking to. Avoid personal e-mail on company time.
- If you send a message containing opinions of yours from a work account, use a disclaimer stating they are your views, and not necessarily your employer's. Humor helps here.
- If you have an academic or nonprofit net account, it's usually best to avoid using it for profit-making activity.

Some rules for "cybertising" (running ads on the net) and success in net-based business:

- Find out what is acceptable. Post only to appropriate forums.
- Learn the accepted rules and codes of conduct for each bboard you intend to place ads on.
- Keep it short and avoid sensationalism.
- Interact with the Internet community on their own terms. When in cyberspace, do as the netters do.

chapter 14

Cybercensorship

Some Censorship Background

Why is censorship becoming an issue on the net when today it seems so free to many netters? It could stem from certain forces that are used to having control over people's communication. Michael Strangelove, in an article about the emerging Electric Gaia, observes that "[t]he ability to communicate to mass audiences has been the privilege of the elite—now it is within the grasp of the person on the street. How governments and international corporations will attempt to control this new power is uncertain, but such power and freedom will certainly not escape the attention of those 'in control' for long. For now, at least, the Internet is the largest uncensored medium of communication in history, and may indeed become the last stand for free speech—an otherwise historically rare phenomenon."

Those who operate net-related services must weigh the "gains" perceived by censoring your customers against potential "fights and flights." That is, some users will either fight you in public (in the real world or over the net), or flee to other services (where they might again flame your service). Neither of these prospects is good for your business.

Chapter 14

Some Anecdotes to Learn From

Case in point: in the recent past, some users of the CompuServe online service claimed they were being censored because they were cut off from playing a popular online game called "Wolfenstein 3-D." It seems there was a possibility that the game's symbolism—which featured swastikas—made it illegal in Germany (which has laws concerning Nazi symbols), and CompuServe was taking no chances. For unrelated reasons, users of the PRODIGY service also recently claimed they were being censored without due cause, which led many members to leave for rival services (and many never returned). Is either service truly a place that doesn't champion free, unrestricted speech, or were they just trying to protect a majority of users? That, like beauty, is in the eye of the beholder—but even if it is not true, the *perception* of a service as leaning toward censorship can be damaging nonetheless.

Ideas and principles from other fields should provide useful insight for developing proper cybermanners in the area of cybercensorship. For example, one might assume that storing sexually explicit magazines or photographs in one's (physical, real) desk at work would very likely be frowned upon by one's employer—and, if publicized, frowned upon by some subset of the other employees. However, a story from the L. A. *Times* (July 12, 1994) told of how "a computer at Lawrence Livermore National Laboratory (LLNL) was being used to store pornographic photographs and distribute them over the Internet." The possible motivations and explanations for such actions will be discussed in greater detail later, but we can make the initial assumption that those involved in this matter at LLNL were not applying the same rules of real-world conduct to their cyberwork realm.

One initial potential explanation for the incident: many netters believe very passionately in cyberfreedom, some even going so far as to claim that "anything goes" on the net. Consider this response from one netter to the *Times* after they broke the story (from a July 21 *Times* article):

"Frankly, why doesn't the idiot media discover that the net is free-form and not run by idealistic, almost communist sounding, writers?"

Are such net users right? Is the electronic universe fundamentally different enough from the real world to warrant a completely different set of ethical codes and behavioral standards? Uncovering the degree of useful overlap between net ethics and real-world rules of conduct is certainly part of the art of cybermanners.

The particular e-mail response quoted above raises another issue. There are many anecdotes of people who would never act as bold in real life as they do in their e-mail language and tone. For example, it is very possible that the creator of the reply message just quoted would never have called the *Times* writer an "idiot" or a "communist" (let alone both) to his face, or even over the phone. If (as argued earlier in the book) this kind of language or tone is more common in electronic messages than those of other media (phone conversations, answering-machine messages, or letters), does that make censorship—or at least some policing of message content—more necessary than in real-world communication? Many netters and cyberrights activists say no, often citing their First Amendment freedom of speech, among other arguments from "real law."

Answers to these and other questions regarding censorship are still very much under debate, but the more netters are aware of them, the greater the chance that democratic decisions can be made if—and when—sweeping "content policies" are ever proposed for the net.

Many long-time netters will always pine for the good old days, and argue that the net was once free, and hence should always be. This is not a good enough argument. For example, motion pictures were once free from conduct codes; many early films were more risqué than is the norm today (well, okay, maybe a lot of "NC-17" and "R" movies are ruder, but that's another matter). But eventually ratings and rules were ushered in that a majority of producers and consumers could live with. The same thing is likely to happen in cyberspace, for better or worse. Stay tuned.

Summary Points

Now let's sort out the main things to remember about online censorship:

- If you run an online system, big or small, weigh the potential gains you may get from censoring some users against the potential fights—and flights from your system—that may ensue. If you are a user choosing an online service, consider past episodes of censorship.

- One can argue that sometimes censoring a few netters may be necessary to protect the larger majority of users. This issue is best resolved on a case-by-case basis, without a sweeping cover-all-bases law.

- As the Internet grows and becomes more like current mainstream media, its rules may approach those of film and television. For advocates of unrestricted free speech, the "good old days" may be gone.

chapter  15

Nethics: Ethical Issues on the Net

Background

What are *nethics*, exactly? Think of it as a kind of big brother to cybermanners. In the majority of cases, manners deal with more detailed and day-to-day matters than ethics. Ethics are usually discussed when broad issues are the concern. To use a real-world example, dating *manners* would involve opening a door for a lady or not—which behavior is correct? Manners of the Fifties would definitely say yes, open the door for her; manners of the Nineties are more unclear and case-by-case. Dating *ethics*, on the other hand, would be invoked for matters such as date rape or date abuse.

Why are nethics important? As is true of other common infrastructures (roads, water reservoirs and delivery systems, and the power generation and distribution network, to name a few), many users worldwide depend on the Internet for the support of their daily research or commercial tasks. The reliable operation of the net and the responsible use of its resources are matters of common interest and concern for its users, operators, and sponsors. Recent events involving the hosts on the Internet (and in similar network

163

infrastructures) underscore the need to reiterate the professional responsibility every Internet user bears to colleagues and to the sponsors of the system. Many of the Internet resources are provided by the U.S. Government, so abuse of the system could become a federal matter above and beyond simple professional cybermanners.

Consider this example of official government policy (observed posted on the Internet itself):

> The Internet is a national facility whose utility is largely a consequence of its wide availability and accessibility. Irresponsible use of this critical resource poses an enormous threat to its continued availability to the technical community.
>
> The U.S. Government sponsors of this system have a fiduciary responsibility to the public to allocate government resources wisely and effectively. Justification for the support of this system suffers when highly disruptive abuses occur. Access to and use of the Internet is a privilege and should be treated as such by all users of this system.
>
> [This organization] strongly endorses the view of the... National Science Foundation Division of Network, Communications Research and Infrastructure which... characterized as unethical and unacceptable any activity which purposely
>
> a. Seeks to gain unauthorized access to the resources of the Internet,
> b. Disrupts the intended use of the Internet,
> c. Wastes resources (people, capacity, computer) through such actions,
> d. Destroys the integrity of computer-based information, and/or
> e. Compromises the privacy of users.
>
> The Internet exists in the general research milieu. Portions of it continue to be used to support research

and experimentation on networking. Because experimentation on the Internet has the potential to affect all of its components and users, researchers have the responsibility to exercise great caution in the conduct of their work. Negligence in the conduct of Internet-wide experiments is both irresponsible and unacceptable.

[We plan] to take whatever actions [we] can, in concert with Federal agencies and other interested parties, to identify and to set up technical and procedural mechanisms to make the Internet more resistant to disruption. Such security, however, may be extremely expensive and may be counterproductive if it inhibits the free flow of information that makes the Internet so valuable. In the final analysis, the health and well-being of the Internet is the responsibility of its users who must, uniformly, guard against abuses which disrupt the system and threaten its long-term viability.

Nethics Rules

That was a mouthful, and okay, I agree with the general spirit of the policy just quoted. But while the passage underscores how important nethics is, I know many readers share my love of lists, so here is a Top Ten tabulation of Computer Ethics Commandments (from the Computer Ethics Institute):

1. Thou shalt not use a computer to harm other people.
2. Thou shalt not interfere with other people's computer work.
3. Thou shalt not snoop around in other people's files.
4. Thou shalt not use a computer to steal.
5. Thou shalt not use a computer to bear false witness.
6. Thou shalt not use or copy software for which you have not paid.

7. Thou shalt not use other people's computer resources without authorization.

8. Thou shalt not appropriate other people's intellectual output.

9. Thou shalt think about the social consequences of the program you write.

10. Thou shalt use a computer in ways that show consideration and respect.

How closely are these being followed today on the net? Hop onto your local online service and see.

Meanwhile, here are more specific nethics rules:

- Don't upload commercial software onto the net.

    If you do, you're probably violating some of the fine print on the envelope your disk came in. If non-paying people get that software from the net, they are stealing by accident.

- Don't steal software from the net.

    Sounds obvious, but even if you're not a renegade hacker, this can happen by mistake. Some people with poorer cybermanners than you may have uploaded commercial software into publicly accessible files that anyone can access. *Remember: just because you can access something on the net doesn't mean it's proper to download it.*

- Don't load viruses onto the net.

    Again, it may seem too simple to mention, but this often happens by accident. Scan your files and take other steps to ensure that anything you send to the net will be virus-free.

Q & A

Q: How can I find out what specific activities are unethical or illegal to do on or over the net?

To find out what *not* to do (a cybermanners endeavor often as important as knowing what *to* do), you can read FAQs for various newsgroups, ask various established net experts (via e-mail), or post questions on relevant bboards.

In general, however, you can assume that many laws that exist in the real world most likely apply to cyberspace as well. For example, since idea exchange is a common activity on the net, those laws that already exist regarding such things as "intellectual property" will apply to net-based creations as well. More specifically, you should assume that the copyright for a book that is stored online for others to read *is still valid* for the electronic version of that book.

Q: *Are there some general rules for "doing the right thing" on the net?*

The Golden Rule never hurt.

Q: *Are there some ethical or legal assumptions I should not make on the net?*

There are some gray areas. For example, it is not clear whether an e-mail message carries all the same legal "baggage" as a real physical letter. And, is there a virtual analog to certified or registered mail (in other words, is a cc:'d message proof of having sent a message to someone)? Not clear.

In general, it might be wise to assume that electronic entities you create will *not* help you in any legal matter—this way you are sure to not get burned. For example, if you are required to contact a certain person by a certain date, or deliver some written material, do *not* assume that an e-mail message will be sufficient—snail mail it as well. Cover your bases.

Q: *How will I know if I commit a form of net-based crime?*

If you get flamed royally, or get your account revoked, that's a sign. Read the FAQs to help prevent behaviors that might indeed be criminal (or *perceived* to be so). Or ask other experienced netters, especially lawyers; legal bboards may help you keep your virtual nose clean.

Summary Points

Nethics is like a "big brother" to "cybermanners": usually more crucial to more people, and more universally accepted.

Remember the Ethics Commandments: Thou shalt...

1. not use a computer to harm other people.
2. not interfere with other people's computer work.
3. not snoop around in other people's files.
4. not use a computer to steal.
5. not use a computer to bear false witness.
6. not use or copy software for which you have not paid.
7. not use other people's computer resources without authorization.
8. not appropriate other people's intellectual output.
9. think about the social consequences of the program you write.
10. use a computer in ways that show consideration and respect.

Some more nethics rules to live by:

- Don't upload commercial software onto the net.
- Don't steal software from the net.
- Don't load viruses onto the net.
- And brush your teeth before bed! This instant!

part IV

Reference

Welcome to the end of the book!

The first appendix is my "Hall of Flame." In it I provide yet another interesting flame form (to supplement those discussed earlier), as well as a summary list of net behaviors that are quite likely to get you flamed. The final pages of this section collect the most important words, phrases, abbreviations and special symbols that relate to concepts presented in earlier chapters. And, of course, what reference section would be complete without an index; you'll find ours at the very end, in a remarkable show of tradition.

Refer to this reference information at any time and in any order. There's no need to read it straight through from start to finish—but if you want to, hey, it's a free country. (Just don't expect any extra credit.) And, before I forget, let me thank you again for reading this book. I hope it's been time well spent, and I hope you'll spread the word and recommend this book to other netters who might benefit from it.

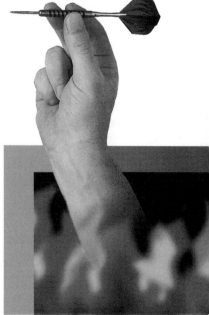

Appendix A

The Hall of Flame

The Form Flame: Another View

Earlier I gave a couple of examples of "form flames," a do-it-yourself way of responding to netters you have a beef with. One was general, the other short and tongue-in-cheek. But now that we're in the nether regions of the appendixes (*appendices* are what give you huge doctor bills if *they* get inflamed) I can share another "form flame" that is a bit less PC—or a bit more PI, depending on your POV. I did not personally create it—but since it was actually posted on the net, it sheds light on how real-world flaming is sometimes expressed. I had to edit some parts out to make it PC enough for this book, but the essence is still present. The X-checked boxes were from the original person who posted this form. Well, enough disclaimers; here goes:

Dear

[ ] [deleted]   [ ] [deleted]   [ ] ignorant snot   [ ] [deleted]

[ ] nerd   [ ] [Elvis]   [ ] [deleted]   [ ] sycophant

[X] retard   [ ] (Name)   [ ] computer geek

171

Appendix A

You are being flamed because you...

[ ] continued a boring useless stupid thread

[ ] repeatedly posted to the same thread that you just posted to

[ ] posted a "test"

[ ] left a whole bunch of editing garbage on the screen

[ ] posted a request for an article which was posted three times in the past week

[ ] posted some sort of... crap that doesn't belong in this group

[X] posted an article that was not funny, but was unoriginal and very boring—and has been posted 6.02×10^{23} times!

[ ] your mother dresses you funny

To recant, you must

[X] actually post a humorous article

[ ] give up all your worldly possessions and become a Tibetan monk

[ ] hang yourself by the big toe for 72 hours

[ ] shave your head, paint a target on it, and go to [a country that hates Americans]

[ ] give your Congressman a donation of three hemp plants to decorate his office

[ ] become politically correct and demand that manholes be renamed to offspring openings

Thank you for the time you have taken to read this, and please desist from the offending behavior that led to this flame. Also, [deleted] OFF!

Wow—some strong sentiment being thrown around there (especially if you could see the unedited version!) — but such is the nature of many areas of the net. Some bboards are definitely not for the squeamish, or for those without a thick skin and a fair amount of stockpiled "idea ammunition."

However, for those who do need to flame once in a while (to let off steam, so to speak), flame forms (or form flames, whatever you prefer) can at least save some time for all parties involved. And they may help prevent flame wars by channeling emotions into predefined units that are, even if PI at times, often tame compared to flames rattled off from scratch in the heat of anger.

Voted "Most Likely to Be Flamed": Top Seven Examples of Flame Bait

These are some actions widely accepted as not-so-great cybermanners—things netters might respond unkindly to. You could also call this "Top Seven Things to Avoid Doing on the Net."

Note that the list has at least one pattern—posts to bboards are almost always more "flammable" than e-mailing one person or a small group—simply because millions could read a bboard post. The list order is not set in stone (Sharon or otherwise), but the general ideas should be clear. Also note that these are not the only examples of flame bait, but hey, you can't make a list too long—"Top Sixty-seven" just doesn't sound sexy.

7. Sending "net-incorrect" e-mail. For instance, one-line test messages, get-rich-quick schemes, dying-child chain letters.

6. Sending "net-correct" (proper in content) e-mail to too many people. For instance, everyone on a long cc: list.

Flammability increases as the number of people sent the e-mail increases, and the less those people are relevant to your message subject.

5. Sending "net-incorrect" e-mail to too many people (i.e., combining the two behaviors just mentioned).

4. Posting a "net-incorrect" message to a bboard.

3. Posting any message ("net-correct" or not) to too many bboards. Flammability increases as the number of bboards sent the post increases, and the less those bboards are related to the topic.

2. Not reading the FAQ before e-mailing or posting a question, when the answer was there in the FAQ for you to find.

1. Engaging in "bad behavior" #2 while also cc:'ing the question to too many people or bboards.

Appendix B

Cyberese

Acronyms and Abbreviations

These are useful to know (they are likely to show up in e-mail and bboard posts you read), and they can help streamline your own messages as well. Pay attention, however, to the audience you are dealing with. For instance, if you are e-mailing someone (e.g., a newbie) who is not likely to understand some acronym you want to use, don't. Or you can always e-mail them with some of these you feel the newbie should know when interacting with you, or e-mail them a glowing endorsement of this book (which its modest author hardly ever plugs).

AKA	Also Known As (for example, "Pres. Clinton AKA Mr. Bill")
BIF	Basis In Fact
BTSOOM	Beats The S**t Out Of Me
BTW	By The Way
FAQ	Frequently Asked Question(s)
FTF or F2F	Face To Face (as in face-to-face meetings)
FUBAR	F****d Up Beyond All Recognition

FWIW	For What It's Worth
FYA	For Your Amusement
FYI	For Your Information
GR&D	Grinning Running & Ducking
IMCO	In My Considered Opinion
IMHO	In My Humble Opinion
IMNSHO	In My Not-So-Humble Opinion
IMO	In My Opinion (let's hear it for simplicity)
IOW	In Other Words
MOTD	Message Of The Day
NBIF	No Basis In Fact
NFW	No F***ing Way
OTOH	On The Other Hand
PC	Politically Correct (or Personal Computer, or IBM's PC, depending on the context)
PI or PIC	Politically Incorrect
PITA	Pain In The A**
POV	Point Of View
RL	Real Life
ROTF,L	Rolling On The Floor, Laughing.
ROTFL	Rolling On The Floor Laughing
RSN	Real Soon Now
RTFM	Read The F***ing Manual (or message) or, Read The Fine Manual (yeah, right!)
RTM	Read The Manual (or message)

Cyberese

SNAFU	Situation Normal, All F****d Up. (A good example of an acronym, because the word itself makes sense—the word *snafu* actually means a situation like the five-word phrase its letters represent. Like FUBAR, this old GI abbreviation now finds renewed use in the virtual trenches of cyberspace.)
SOL	S**t Out of Luck
TIA	Thanks In Advance
TIC	Tongue In Cheek
unPC	A cute way of saying the same thing as PI. (Also good to use if you are e-mailing a Private Investigator, since these Magnum wannabes probably think they alone can use PI; but then, how often do you really e-mail a fictional guy like Magnum?)
WTH	What The Heck
YMMV	Your Mileage May Vary
[TM]	TradeMark

Now here's a selection of acronyms recommended by the "soc.singles" newsgroup on USENET:

FOAF	Friend Of A Friend
LAFS	Love At First Sight (or, "Love At First Site" for those in a hurry.)
LDR	Long Distance Relationship
LJBF	Let's Just Be Friends (now considered a verb)
LO	Lust Object (occasionally also Love Object)

Appendix B

LTR	Long Term Relationship
MOTAS	Member Of The Appropriate Sex
MOTIS	Member Of The Inappropriate Sex
MOTOS	Member Of The Opposite Sex
MOTSS	Member Of The Same Sex
NG	Nice Guy/Gal
NIFOC	Nude In Front Of Computer
PDA	Public Display of Affection
POM	Problem Older Man
POSSLQ	Person of Opposite Sex Sharing Living Quarters
POW	Problem Older Woman
PYM	Problem Younger Man (also Problem Younger Mutant)
PYW	Problem Younger Woman
RI	Romantic Interest
RP	Romantic Partner
SMV	Sexual Market Value
SNAG	Sensitive New-Age Guy
SO	Significant Other
TL&EH	True Love & Eternal Happiness
WFYITBWNBLJO	Waiting For You In The Bathtub Wearing Nothing But Lime Jell-O. (Oh yeah, I'm sure you'll use this as often as the word "the.")

Emoticons

As you've read earlier, there are not a lot of ways to add extra emotion to your electronic messages, above and beyond the wonderful prose all your poetic netters use (especially some flamers—some of them almost approach Jack-Kerouac-ian brilliance).

However, emoticons are one welcome exception. They can be used to convey humor, sadness, silliness, whimsy, anger, and in general show you have a fun side.

You read emoticons by tilting your head (or your mind) to the left. (No, they were not invented by someone who was a pain in the neck—they look this way due to the limitations of computer characters.)

Should you use these all the time? Perhaps not—it's really up to you. If writing an official memo to your boss or some other business colleague, you might want to stick to words only. That is, sometimes you can use creative word usage to get the same point across as an emoticon would. Emoticons help clarify shades of meaning, but remember that making your *words* clear helps even more.

Here's a selection of emoticons, along with their common names and/or descriptions:

:-)	Smile, smiley, or happy face (indicating humor). The most popular emoticon by far.
:)	a noseless smiley (or *sans nose* if you speak Frenglish)
:.)	a small-skewed-button-nosed smiley
8-)	smile from someone wearing glasses
B-)	another version
:->	ironic or devious smile
;-)	yet another happy face; a knowing smile (winking, which means there may be a devilish side to your words)
:-.)	a happy face with a beauty mark on the upper lip (e.g., a Cindy-Crawford-type model)

Appendix B

:-(	the anti-smiley (frown, that is; let down, sad)
>:-(	someone mad or annoyed
|:-|	I am not impressed (or "no reaction")
>:-)	evil grin (could use after tricking someone or saying something a bit devilish or controversial)
:-Q	sticking your tongue out at the reader
:-()	a big mouth (e.g., when you feel you rambled on)
:-O	surprised face (or a big mouth, or Mick Jagger, who is often online on DELPHI, by the way)
@>—,—'-	a rose (sometimes useful in virtual dating)
xxooxxoo	love & kisses (which, like the rose, is great for date mail)

Note that another way to convey emotion is to put the actual emotion, or the first letter of its name, into [brackets].

For example, a smiley's meaning could be conveyed as [g] or [grin], frown as [f] or [frown], etc. This method can give you even greater shades of meaning, since you can convey all the meaning expressed in emoticons in equivalent words/letters—but not vice versa (that is, there are some word combinations that are too hard to make into emoticons).

Using the [bracketing] alternative to convey emotion or feeling is best when you absolutely have to be clear about meaning, or are afraid of hurting feelings through misunderstanding. Emoticons are best when you want quick, shorthand emotional "punctuation."

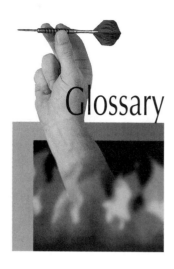

Glossary

The Neat Net Set

Definitions (Words, Phrases, Abbreviations)

America Online (AOL)   A commercial online service which provides some Internet access features (e.g., e-mail, USENET, and others to be added soon).

ASCII   In a word, text. For instance, if someone asks you to "just e-mail the ASCII file," they mean a text file (often stated when there is formatting in the original file; since formatting often becomes garbage when sent over e-mail, ASCII versions tend to work better). More specifically: letters A (or a) to Z (or z), numbers, and some other assorted miscellaneous characters.

bandwidth   The virtual size of the virtual lanes of the net "highway." Not really a defined word; more of a metaphor for net activities. Often used in a problem sense, as in "you're using up valuable bandwidth with your irrelevant flame—get a life!"

bulletin board (AKA *bboard*)   Although several meanings exist in the computer world, I use this term to represent the virtual space to which netters send messages for other netters to read and respond to. So named because the virtual space exhibits the features of real world bulletin boards: multiple people can post notes on them, and just as many people can stop by and read them. Synonym: *newsgroup* (on *USENET*).

channel   A path over which messages can be transmitted. Usually used in reference to *chatting* ("chat channel"). Channels may be secure or insecure, and may have eavesdroppers (or enemies, or disrupters, etc.) who alter messages, insert and delete messages, and so on. Cryptography is a means by which communications over insecure channels are protected.

chatting   Talking to another netter over the net. For instance, IRC on the Internet lets users talk over channels that can be created or destroyed by the users; many users can chat over the same channel. I use this term to cover all the forms of interactive communication on various net services—such as using CB on CompuServe, IRC on the Internet, and so on. The Internet "talk" program is like a more limited version of chatting (only one-to-one).

CompuServe   A commercial online service which provides some Internet access features (e.g., e-mail).

cybermanners   Manners that relate to activities conducted in cyberspace (e.g., on the net). In most cases it is identical in meaning to *netiquette*, although cybermanners can also be used to cover manners or etiquette for non-net-related computer matters. (*Cyber* is a general prefix relating to computers and automation.)

compumatch (AKA *computer match*)   A romantic match, such as those made during online dating or cybersex activities.

crossposting   Sending the same message to multiple bboards. If overdone, a *cybernono*.

cyberspace (AKA *cyberverse*)   Often used as a nickname for the *Internet*; or, the electronic domain; computer-generated spaces. Some say it is the "consensual reality" described in *Neuromancer*. Others say the phone system is an example.

cybersurfers   Netters who ride bitstream waves to crisscross the net.

cybertising   *Cyber*ese for Internet adver*tising*; broadcasting sales pitches in cyberspace. Okay, it's a term not in wide use yet, but hopefully it will be—go out and use it, it's catchy!

decrypt   The inverse of *encrypt*. Another synonym: decode. As in "I can't decrypt this darn message—I've heard of privacy, but this is ridiculous!"

DELPHI   Yet another commercial online service, which heavily advertises its Internet access features. Unlike most other commercial services, DELPHI can offer users more "full service" (access to more net features)—though others (as of mid-1994) are catching up.

dictionary flame   A post correcting someone's definition or use of a word. Sometimes the flamer's initial intentions are good—to help someone learn—but this person's "teacher" side gets carried away with language and tone (e.g., becomes condescending).

digital pseudonym (AKA *crypto identity*)   A way for individuals to set up accounts with various organizations without revealing more information than they wish; hence, a means to enhance netter privacy.

e-mail (AKA *electronic mail*)   The virtual world analog to *snailmail*. (n.) A message sent to another *netter* over the Internet. (v.) To send e-mail. I know, it sounds circular, but it ain't, trust me :-).

e-mailbox (AKA *electronic mailbox*)   Where e-mail is received and/or stored (and/or forgotten!).

encrypt   Change a *plaintext* message into a coded one, often used to enhance one's privacy by making one's message more "snoop-proof." For example, there are ways to ensure that only certain people can decode your encrypted message (for instance, giving your friends a kind of digital key that must be used in order to do the decoding). The actual techniques used to encrypt are called *encryption* methods.

Glossary

FAQ *(FAQs)*   Frequently Asked Question(s). Often refers to the FAQ of a particular bboard. Most bboards have FAQs so that endlessly repeated questions do not clog the net; *newbies* can just look up the answer in the FAQ. If a FAQ is not present on a bboard today, chances are it will be reposted in the near future, or you can access it from a computer archive site via *FTP*, *Gopher*, or other search-and-retrieve methods.

flame   An emotional, often personal attack on another person's article. The statement, "I disagree with your statement because of X" is not a flame, whereas "I disagree with your moronic statement and the fact that you would say such a thing proves you're a complete idiot" is.

flame bait (AKA *flamebait*)   Apt to attract a *flame*. Something posted publicly that appears designed to inspire flames; usually this is a post that is not only likely to annoy a lot of people, but is also worded in such a way as to arouse the ire of readers.

flame war   When flames start firing back and forth between two or more netters—either via e-mail, or over bulletin boards (which is an even more flammable situation).

forum   I use this term as synonymous with "bboard." However, users of some commercial online services like CompuServe use this word exclusively for their species of bboards.

FTP (AKA *anonymous FTP*)   File transfers to and from other sites on the net.

GEnie   Yet another commercial online service.

GIF, or .GIF   This abbrev stands for "Graphics Interchange Format" and is a common format in which pictures are stored for display on a computer screen. When discussions turn visual, some netters might offhandedly ask for a "GIF"—but even if you're asked for one, it is generally considered poor cybermanners to post GIFs to newsgroups, because these files tend to be quite large.

guide   Someone from a net service provider who monitors areas of the service (e.g., public chat rooms) to ensure proper conduct. Sometimes referred to as a *cybercop*, *monitor*, or *room monitor*.

hir Gender-neutral pronoun equivalent to "him or her" or possessive pronoun equivalent to "his or her" (alternate spelling: "zie" and "zir").

impostor A netter who, using a fake online persona, posts messages on bboards. Impostors usually want to generate responses by stating facts or opinions that are either untrue, unproven, or misleading. The goal is often financial gain.

Internet The "network of networks" that links people around the world in a global village, a massive communication network. Mostly text-based communication today, this should change in the near future (e.g., voice-mail may replace or supplement e-mail). Also referred to as "information highway," "cyberspace," or "the embryonic beginning of a new massive globally linked transpersonal superconsciousness." Wow.

jamming What happens when an above-average amount of noise is present over a part of the net. For example, if someone crossposts to too many newsgroups, jamming has occurred. The type of jamming that occurs when there is noise interference on radio waves is one analogy to this. I sometimes refer to "jamming the netwaves," which draws on this metaphor.

kill (v.) or **killfile** (n.) Most newsreaders have a provision for "killing" messages; that is, marking them as read before you get to them, so your newsreader then skips over them automatically instead of showing them to you. Keep in mind, however, that most topics die or change over time; unless you edit that line out of your killfile it will continue to live in there, eating up processor time and generally slowing everything down whenever you read that group—poor cybermanners, indeed. In general, it is good cybermanners to keep your killfiles to a minimum, especially if you are sharing a computer with other users.

lurker User who reads bboard groups but never posts to them.

185

mailing list Refers to mailing-list discussion groups. In general, it works like this: you add your name to a mailing list that contains many names of like-minded people. After this process of *subscribing* to such a list, a server machine periodically e-mails documents dealing with the topic of that list to all subscribers.

net Short for "the Internet."

nethics Condensation of "net ethics." A kind of "big brother" to cybermanners.

netiquette Net etiquette. In most cases I assume it is identical in meaning to cybermanners.

newbie New netter. Sometimes more generally used for people who either *are* new to the cyberworld, or just *act* like they are. For example, someone may refer to you as a newbie in an e-mail message even if you've been online for months or years. Multiply the number of months you've been on the net *times* the number of "newbie" references you receive from others; the result is what I call your *embarrassment factor*—and the number of times you should read this book ;-).

newsgroup I use this term as synonymous with *bboard*. However, most Internet users call bboards "newsgroups," and those on some commercial online services like CompuServe call them *forums*.

newsreader Program that you use to read bboard (e.g., USENET) posts.

offline Somewhere outside of (off) the net. For instance, if you're on a chat channel and someone suggests "Let's meet offline," they want to actually meet you in the flesh (but don't get fresh; remember your *real* manners after you go offline).

online On the net, somewhere, in some capacity. Some also use the more slangy/sexy term "jacked in" to convey the same meaning, but "online" covers more situations and is more widely used. For example, an "online newspaper" is one that is distributed over the net.

PC and **PCness** Politically correct and political correctness. (I will ignore PC's "personal computer" interpretation for a moment.) PCness has in recent years gathered a strong following, but even more recently has led to a strong backlash as well, especially on the net, which often seems more unPC, or PI. Like any democracy, the net's population is composed of various factions that have differing opinions; in some areas, PCness seems mandatory, while others may treat you strangely if you act that way. Sending a PC message is your safest bet, while acting PI is more likely to cause flaming behavior directed your way. But you must use your judgment.

plaintext (AKA *cleartext*) Original text of a message; text that is to be encrypted—or, the original recovered message after decryption has been performed.

plan file Also referred to simply as a *.plan* or *plan*, they typically contain details about the person who created and owns that file. The usual content: full name, affiliation, interests, and often real world address and phone information. The main use for plan files is to give other netters a chance to find out more about you without having to repeatedly answer introductory or investigative queries.

post (n.) The message you sent to the bboard. (v.) To send the message.

PRODIGY Another online service. After getting flak for some alleged censoring of certain users, it is now perceived in certain circles as more conservative than its net competitors. Others disagree. PRODIGY does give free initial online time (as many online services do), so check it out, and as always, decide for yourself!

roadkill on the information superhighway Much-overused expression (now cliché) referring to netters who, for various reasons, wind up unhappy, dissatisfied, or even forced off of the net. Reading this book, following FAQs, asking politely for help in the right place when needed—all will help you avoid becoming roadkill.

Glossary

sie Gender-neutral pronoun equivalent to "she or he." Another way to convey the same intent: "s/he." Gender neutrality is usually considered PC on the net.

signature (AKA *sig* or *.sig*) "Signature," a short, standardized message tacked on to the end of all one's posts; usually one to four lines of text, containing one's e-mail address, employer, favorite quote, and/or other pertinent (or impertinent) personal information.

snailmail (AKA *snail mail*) The real-world analog to e-mail; the normal through-rain-and-snow postal service. (Snail implies slow, in case you're slow. But now I know you're in the know!)

spelling flame Related to dictionary flame; a post correcting a previous article's spelling in a showy fashion, as a sneaky means of belittling the person or undermining the article's content, instead of actually responding to that content.

spoofing (AKA *masquerading*) Posing as another netter. Used by those unethical (or un-nethical, if you prefer) folks who steal passwords, modify files, and take other actions that exhibit extremely awful cybermanners, to say the least. New kinds of digital signatures and other authentication methods are being developed to help prevent this.

sysadmin System administrator; a kind of local net authority figure—though one should not assume a sysadmin can act to control the actions of other netters (e.g., those who show poor cybermanners) as easily or forcefully as a real policeperson. Each sysadmin manages a particular (online computer-based) site on the net—one of the individual networks that make up the Internet "network of networks."

Telnet A program which allows netters to visit other sites on the net. Once you have "Telnetted" to a remote site, you can usually perform most the actions on that site that its regular users can—though more and more sites are adding restrictions to help enhance security.

trolling A fishing metaphor; usually refers to how advertisers "troll" the net with alluring ads as "bait" to "reel in" some buyers. Many netters dislike this behavior, considering it poor cybermanners to use the net for such purposes. Business folk often disagree. The issue is not yet resolved, and may never be.

usenetizen (AKA *USENETizen*)   A citizen (or denizen, if you prefer "d" words) of the USENET bboard cyberverse. One who uses USENET.

usenetter (AKA *USENETter*)   A *netter* who participates in the USENET bboard system. Variation: *usenetizen*.

virtual sex (or *v-sex*)   Sex that takes place in virtual reality—for the purposes of this book, this generally means in text form. For instance, exchanging thoughts on sex over bboards, or more intimate lines of dialogue over public or private chat channels.

Index

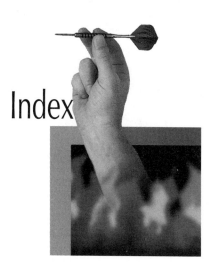

A

abbreviations (cyberese), 7-12, 43-45, 175-178
accounts
  disk space, managing, 72-73
  security, 145-147
addicts, 110-112
addresses (e-mail), 3-5
advertising, 183, 188
  bboards, 64, 94-96, 152-156
  e-mail, 157
America Online, 181
anonymity, 61, 104-105
automated e-mail replies, 114-115

B

bandwidths, 46, 181
bboards, 41, 45, 49-50, 181
  abbreviations, 43-45
  advertising, 64, 94-96, 152-156
  commercial online services, 42
  communities, 141-142
  cybersex, 124
  FAQs (Frequently Asked Questions), 45
  flames, 88-92
  jamming, 96-101, 185
  lurking, 47, 55-56, 185
  mailing lists, 76-77, 186
  postings, 42-43, 47, 187
  USENET bboards, 41-42, 45
blind cc: (e-mail), 146
bulletin boards, *see* bboards
business, 149-152
  e-mail, 37-38, 145, 150, 156
  advertising, 152-157

C

cc:s (carbon copies) (e-mail), 25, 36-37, 146
celebrities
  chat, 122
  e-mail, 97-98, 144
  fake identities, 104-105
censorship, 143-144, 159
  cases, 160-162
  cybersex, 144, 160
chain letters (bboards), 52
chameleonymous, 104-105
channels (chat), 121, 182
chat, 121-124, 182
  BITNET Relay, 120
  celebrities, 122
  channels, 121, 182
  cybersex, 124-130
    FAQs (frequently asked questions), 130-131
    guides, 127-130
    opening lines, 125
    rooms, 126-130
  dating, 130-131
  F2F (face-to-face) meetings, 120-121, 123

191

flames, 123
handles, 122
IRC (Internet Relay Chat), 120
paging users, 122
personalities, 123
community bboards, 141-142
compumatches, 182
CompuServe, 182
   CB, 120
   censorship, 160
   forums, 184
Computer Ethics Institute, 165-166
conferencing, 37
Cook, John, 120-121
copyrights
   e-mail, 35
   FTP (file transfer protocol), 75
crossposting (bboards), 47, 64, 66, 182
cyberese, 7-12, 43-45, 175-178
cybersex, 189
   bboards, 124
   censorship, 144, 160
   chat, 124-130
      guides, 127-130
      opening lines, 125
      rooms, 126-130
   compumatches, 182
cyberspace, 182
cybersurfers, 183
cybertising, 183

D

dating, 130-131, 182
decrypting, 183
DELPHI, 183
dictionary flames, 46, 183
digital pseudonyms, 183

E

E-Ads, 157
e-mail, 17-21, 37-39, 183
   abbreviations (cyberese), 7-12
   addresses, 3-5
   advertising, 157

bboards, posting, 51
blind cc:, 146
businesses, 37-38, 145, 150, 156
celebrities, 97-98, 144
conferencing, 37
copyrights, 35
emoticons, 12-14
flames, 83-84, 88-90
license agreements, 35
mail bombs, 101
mailboxes, 183
   jamming, 96-101, 185
   organizing, 72
mailing lists, 37, 76-77, 186
mass mailings, 38
messages
   automated reply messages, 114-115
   cc:s (carbon copies), 36-37
   emotional passages, 31
   encrypting, 147
   deleting, 147
   formality, 30-31
   forwarding, 36-37
   headers, 6, 24-26
   humor, 31
   interpreting, 34-35
   plagerism, 35
   privacy, 144-147
   proofreaders, 33
   quotations, 35-36
   receiving e-mail intended for someone else, 34
   sarcasm, 31
   sending, 37-38
   shouting, 30
   signatures, 7, 11, 32-33
   writing, 5-7, 21-24, 26, 28-32
E-Mail of the Rich and Famous, 97
Ebert, Roger, 144
Electronic Wild West, 82
emoticons, 12-14, 178-180
encrypting, 183
   e-mail, 147
   postings (bboards), 59, 62
ethics, 163-166, 186
   software use, 165-166
   viruses, 166

F

F2F (face-to-face meetings), 120-121, 123
fake identities, 104-105
FAQs (frequently asked questions), 8-45, 184
file transfer protocol, *see* FTP
files
  graphics files, 47, 184
  plan files, 187
flame wars, 11, 184
Flame Wars, 125
flames, 10, 82-84, 88-90, 184
  avoiding, 84-88
  bboards, 89-90
  chat, 123
  dictionary flames, 46, 183
  e-mail, 83-84
  filtering, 84-87
  flamebait, 46, 184
  flame forms, 90-92, 171-174
  flame wars, 11, 184
  grammar flames, 52
  responses, 84-87
  spelling flames, 47, 188
forums, *see* bboards
forwarding e-mail, 36-37
FTP (file transfer protocol), 74-75, 184

G-H-I

gender issues, 11, 185, 134-138
GEnie, 184
GIF (graphics interchange format) files, 47, 184
government regulation, *see* regulation (Internet)
grammar flames, 52
graphics files, 47, 184
guides (chat), 127-130, 184

handles (chat), 122, 134
hangouts, 141
headers
  e-mail, 6, 24-26
  postings (bboards), 57-66

help
  bboard help requests, 37
  e-mail, 39
  FTP (file transfer protocol), 75

imposters, 185
Internet, 164-165, 185
IRC (Internet Relay Chat), 120

J-K-L

jamming, 96-101, 185

licensing agreements
  e-mail, 35
  FTP (file transfer protocol), 75
lurking, 47, 185
  bboards, 55-56
  chat channels, 121

M-N-O

mail bombs, 101
mailboxes, *see* e-mail, mailboxes
mailing lists, 37, 76-77, 186
mass postings, *see* spamming
meeting people, 139-141

nethics, *see* ethics
netiquette, 186
network security, 147
newbies, 10, 112-113, 186
news (bboards), posting, 52
newsgroups, *see* bboards; USENET bboards
newsreaders (USENET bboards), 45, 48, 186

offline, 186
online, 186

P

paging users (chat), 122
passwords, 145-147
people, *see* users
plagerism (e-mail), 35
plaintext files, 187

plan file, 187
pornography, 160
postings (bboards), 47, 187
  anonymity, 61
  audience, 53-55
  crossposting, 64-66, 182
  e-mail, 51
  encrypting, 59, 62
  FAQs (frequently asked questions), 66-70
  headers, 57-58, 66
  mass postings, *see* spamming
  posting, 64-66
  quotations, 62
  signatures, 64
  spamming, 94-96
  spoilers, 62
  unacceptable postings, 50-53
  writing, 56-62
privacy (e-mail), 144-147
Prodigy, 160, 187
pseudonyms, 104, 183
  chat, 122
  gender issues, 134

Q-R

questions, *see* FAQs (frequently asked questions)

receiving e-mail intended for someone else, 34
regulation (Internet), 164-165
Relay (BITNET), 120
rooms (chat), 126-130

S

security (networks), 147-147
sending
  e-mail
    cc:s (carbon copies), 36-37
    business messages, 37-38
    groups, 38
  postings (bboards) 64-66
sex, *see* cybersex; virtual sex
shouting, 30

signatures, 188
  e-mail messages, 7, 11, 32-33
  postings (bboards), 64
smileys, 12-14, 178-180
snail-mail, 11, 188
spamming, 94-96
spelling flames, 47, 52, 188
spoofing, 188
subscriptions to mailing lists, 76-77
sysadmin (system administrator), 188

T-U

talk, *see* chat
telnet, 73-74, 188
trolling, 188

USENET bboards, 41-42, 45, 49-50
  abbreviations, 43-45
  advertising, 64, 152-156
  cybersex, 124
  FAQs (Frequently Asked Questions), 45
  flames, 89-92
  jamming, 96-101, 185
  lurking, 47, 55-56, 185
  mailing lists, 76-77, 186
  newsreaders, 45, 48, 186
  postings, 47, 187
USENETizens, 46, 189
user accounts, *see* accounts

V-Z

virtual hangouts, 141
virtual sex, 189
viruses, 165-166
  FTP files, 75

whamming, 101-102
Wolfenstein 3-D, 160